Fodor's®

Pocket
Munich

P9-BZF-317

Excerpted from *Fodor's Germany*

Fodor's Travel Publications, Inc.
New York • Toronto • London • Sydney • Auckland
www.fodors.com

Fodor's Pocket Munich

EDITORS: Alison B. Stern, Audra Epstein

Editorial Contributors: David Brown, Helayne Schiff, Marshall Schwartz-mann (Gold Guide editor), Robert Tilley

Editorial Production: Linda K. Schmidt

Maps: David Lindroth, *cartographer*; Robert Blake, *map editor*

Design: Fabrizio La Rocca, *creative director*; Guido Caroti, *associate art director*; Lyndell Brookhouse-Gil, *cover design;* Jolie Novak, *photo editor*

Production/Manufacturing: Mike Costa

Cover Photograph: Walter Bibikow/The Viesti Collection, Inc.

Copyright

Second Edition

ISBN 0–679–00051–8

Special Sales

Fodor's Travel Publications are available at special discounts for bulk purchases for sales promotions or premiums. Special editions, including personalized covers, excerpts of existing guides, and corporate imprints, can be created in large quantities for special needs. For more information, contact your local bookseller or write to Special Markets, Fodor's Travel Publications, 201 East 50th Street, New York, NY 10022. Inquiries from Canada should be directed to your local Canadian bookseller or sent to Random House of Canada, Ltd., Marketing Department, 2775 Matheson Boulevard East, Mississauga, Ontario L4W 4P7. Inquiries from the United Kingdom should be sent to Fodor's Travel Publications, 20 Vauxhall Bridge Road, London SW1V 2SA, England.

PRINTED IN THE UNITED STATES OF AMERICA

10 9 8 7 6 5 4 3 2 1

CONTENTS

ON THE ROAD WITH FODOR'S

WHEN I PLAN a vacation, the first thing I do is survey my friends and colleagues to find someone who's just been where I'm going. That's because there's no substitute for a recommendation from a good friend who knows your tastes, your budget, and your circumstances, someone who's just been there. Unfortunately, such friends are few and far between. So it's nice to know that there's *Fodor's Pocket Munich.*

In the first place, this book won't stay home when you hit the road. It will accompany you every step of the way, steering you away from wrong turns and wrong choices and never expecting a thing in return. Most important of all, it's written and assiduously updated by the kind of people you *would* hit up for travel tips if you knew them. They're as choosy as your pickiest friend, except they've probably seen a lot more of Munich. In these pages, they don't send you chasing down every neighborhood and sight in Munich but have instead selected the best ones, the ones that are worthy of your time and money. To make it easy for you to put it all together in the time you have, they've created short itineraries and neighborhood walks that you can mix and match in a snap.

About Our Writer

Our success in helping to make your trip the best of all possible vacations is a credit to the hard work of our extraordinary writers.

Robert Tilley landed in Germany more than 25 years ago, intending to stay a year. German women were responsible for his extended stay—he married one, who's now a seasoned Fodor's researcher. Robert runs a media company in Munich and writes in a lakeside hideaway in the Bavarian Alps. His branch office is in a local brewery cellar.

We'd also like to thank Helga Brenner-Khan, of the German National Tourist Office, and the German Wine Information Bureau.

Connections

We're pleased that the American Society of Travel Agents continues to endorse Fodor's as its guidebook of choice. ASTA is the world's largest and most influential travel trade association, operating in more than 170 countries, with 27,000 members pledged to adhere to a strict code of ethics reflecting the Society's motto, "Integrity in Travel." ASTA shares Fodor's devotion to providing smart, honest travel information and advice to travelers, and we've long recommended that our readers—even those who have guidebooks and traveling friends—consult ASTA member agents for the experience and professionalism they bring to your vacation planning.

On Fodor's Web site (www.fodors.com), check out the new Resource Center, an on-line companion to the Essential Information chapter of this book, complete with useful hot links to related sites. In our forums, you can also get lively advice from other travelers and more great tips from Fodor's experts worldwide.

How to Use This Book

Organization

Up front is **Essential Information,** an easy-to-use section arranged alphabetically by topic. Under each listing you'll find tips and information that will help you accomplish what you need to in Munich. You'll also find addresses and telephone numbers of organizations and companies that offer destination-related services and detailed information and publications.

The first chapter in the guide, Destination: Munich, helps get you in the mood for your trip. Pleasures and Pastimes describes the activities and sights that make Munich unique, while Festivals and Seasonal Events alerts you to special events you'll want to seek out.

Chapter 2 is subdivided by neighborhood; each subsection recommends a walking or driving tour and lists sights alphabetically. The remaining chapters are arranged in alphabetical order by subject (dining, lodging, nightlife and the arts, outdoor activities and sports, shopping, and side trips from Munich). At the end of the book you'll find a brief introduction to the German language, along with a glossary of common terms and menu items.

Icons and Symbols

★ Our special recommendations
✕ Restaurant
🏠 Lodging establishment
🐤 Good for kids (rubber duck)
☞ Sends you to another section of the guide for more information
✉ Address
☎ Telephone number
☉ Opening and closing times
💰 Admission prices (those we give apply to adults; substantially reduced fees are almost always available for children, students, and senior citizens)

Numbers in white and black circles ③ ❸ that appear on the maps, in the margins, and within the tours correspond to one another.

Hotel Facilities

We always list the facilities that are available—but we don't specify whether you'll be charged extra to use them: When pricing accommodations, always ask what's included—assume that all rooms have private baths unless noted otherwise. In addition, when you book a room, be sure to mention if you have a disability or are traveling with children, if you prefer a private bath or a certain type of bed, or if you have specific dietary needs or other concerns.

Assume that hotels operate on the **European Plan** (EP, with no meals) unless we specify that they use the **Continental Plan** (CP, with a Continental breakfast daily), **Breakfast Plan** (BP, with a full breakfast daily), **Modified American Plan** (MAP, with breakfast and dinner daily), or the **Full American Plan** (FAP, with all meals).

Restaurant Reservations and Dress Codes

Reservations are always a good idea; we mention them only when they're essential or are not accepted. Book as far ahead as you can, and reconfirm as soon as you arrive. Unless otherwise noted, the restaurants listed are open daily for lunch and dinner. We mention dress only when men are required to wear a jacket or a jacket and tie. Look for an overview of local dining-out habits in the Pleasures and Pastimes section of Chapter 1.

Credit Cards

The following abbreviations are used: **AE**, American Express; **D**, Discover; **DC**, Diners Club; **MC**, MasterCard; and **V**, Visa.

Don't Forget to Write

You can use this book in the confidence that all prices and opening times are based on information supplied to us at press time; Fodor's cannot accept responsibility for any errors. Time inevitably brings changes, so always confirm information when it matters—especially if you're making a detour to visit a specific place.

Were the restaurants we recommended as described? Did our hotel picks exceed your expectations? Did you find a museum we recommended a waste of time? Keeping a travel guide fresh and up-to-date is a big job, and we welcome your feedback, positive *and* negative. If you have complaints, we'll look into them and revise our entries when the facts warrant it. If you've discovered a special place that we haven't included, we'll pass the information along to our correspondents and have them check it out. So send us your thoughts via e-mail at editors@fodors.com (specifying the name of the book on the subject line) or on paper in care of the *Pocket Munich* editor at Fodor's, 201 East 50th Street, New York, New York 10022. In the meantime, have a wonderful trip!

Karen Cure

Karen Cure
Editorial Director

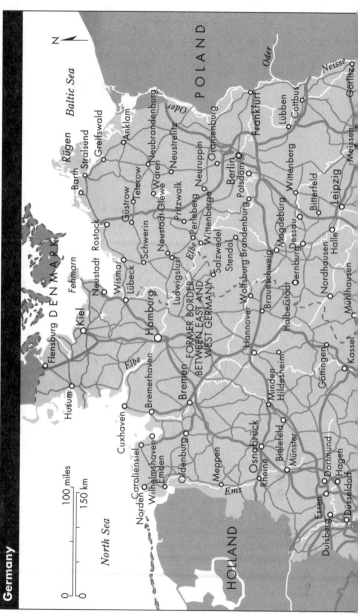

Germany

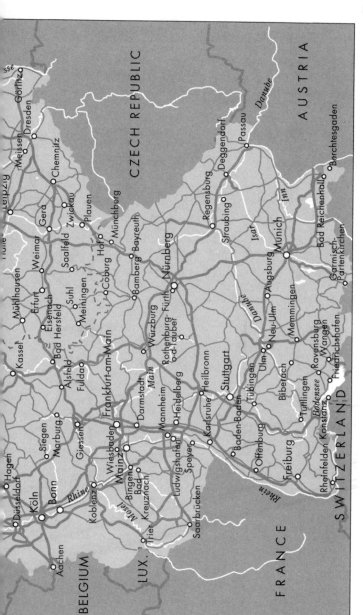

Munich Public Transit System

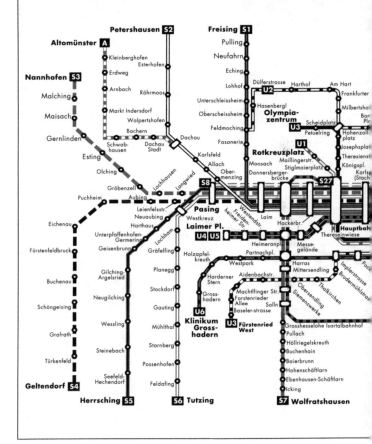

U6 Garching-Hochbrück
- Fröttmaning
- Kieferngarten
- Freimann
- Studentenstadt
- Alte Heide
- Nordfriedhof
- Dietlindenstr.
- Münchener Freiheit
- Giselastrasse
- Universität
- Odeonsplatz
- Lehel

Arabellapark **U4**
- Richard-Strauss-Str.
- Böhmerwaldplatz
- Prinzregentenplatz
- Max-Weber-Platz

S8 Flughafen München
- Ismaning
- Unterföhring
- Johanneskirchen
- Englschalking
- Daglfing
- Leuchtenbergring

U2 U-Bahn
S1 S-Bahn

S6 Erding
- Altenerding
- Aufhausen
- St Kolomann
- Ottenhofen
- Markt Schwaben
- Poing
- Grub
- Heimstetten
- Feldkirchen
- Riem

S3 **S5** **S7** Ostbahnhof

Berg am Laim
- Trudering
- Gronsdorf
- Haar
- Vaterstetten
- Baldham
- Zorneding
- Eglharting
- Kirchseeon
- Grafing Bahnhof
- Grafing Stadt

S4 Ebersberg

- Isartor
- Marienplatz
- Rosenheimerpl.
- Untersbergstrasse
- StMartinstrasse

U1 Innsbrucker Ring
- Michaelibad
- Quiddestrasse
- Neuperlach Zentrum
- Therese-Giehse-Allee
- Neuperlach Süd
- Neubiberg
- Ottobrunn
- Hohenbrunn
- Wächterhof
- Höhenkirchen-Siegertsbrunn
- Dürrnhaar
- Aying
- Peiss
- Grosshelfendorf

S1 Kreuzstrasse

- Fraunhoferstr.
- Kolumbuspl.
- Silberhornstr.
- Giesing
- Karl-Preis-Platz
- Perlach
- Fasangarten
- Fasangarten
- Unterhaching
- Taufkirchen-U
- Furth

U2 **U5**
Neuperlach Süd

S27
Deisenhofen
- Sauerlach
- Otterfing

Holzkirchen **S2**

- Goetheplatz
- Sendlinger Tor

ESSENTIAL INFORMATION

Basic Information on Traveling in Munich, Savvy Tips to Make Your Trip a Breeze, and Companies and Organizations to Contact

AIR TRAVEL

BOOKING YOUR FLIGHT

Price is just one factor to consider when booking a flight: frequency of service and even a carrier's safety record are often just as important. Major airlines offer the greatest number of departures. Smaller airlines—including regional and no-frills airlines—usually have a limited number of flights daily. On the other hand, so-called low-cost airlines usually are cheaper, and their fares impose fewer restrictions, such as advance-purchase requirements. Safety-wise, low-cost carriers as a group have a good history—about equal to that of major carriers.

When you book, **look for nonstop flights** and **remember that "direct" flights stop at least once.** Try to **avoid connecting flights,** which require a change of plane. Two airlines may jointly operate a connecting flight, so ask if your airline operates every segment—you may find that your preferred carrier flies you only part of the way. International flights on a country's flag carrier are almost always nonstop; U.S. airlines often fly direct.

Ask your airline if it offers electronic ticketing, which eliminates all paperwork. There's no ticket to pick up or misplace. You go directly to the gate and give the agent your confirmation number—a real blessing if you've lost your ticket or made last-minute changes in travel plans. There's no worry about waiting in line at the airport while precious minutes tick by.

CARRIERS

➤ MAJOR AIRLINES: **Continental** (☎ 800/525–0280). **Delta** (☎ 800/221–1212). **Lufthansa** (☎ 800/645–3880). **United** (☎ 800/ 241–6522). **US Airways** (☎ 800/ 428–4322).

➤ SMALLER AIRLINES: **LTU International Airways** (☎ 800/888–0200) is a German company with direct flights to Dusseldorf and connections to Munich. Flights depart from Fort Myers, Miami and Orlando, and seasonally from New York and Los Angeles.

➤ FROM THE U.K.: **British Airways** (☎ 0345/222–111). **Lufthansa** (✉ 10 Old Bond St., London W1X 4EN, ☎ 0181/ 750–3300 or 0345/737–747). **Air UK** (☎ 0345/666–777).

CHARTERS

Charters usually have the lowest fares but are the least dependable. Departures are infrequent and seldom on time, flights can be delayed for up to 48 hours or can be canceled for any reason up to 10 days before you're scheduled to leave. Itineraries and prices can change after you've booked your flight.

In the U.S., the Department of Transportation's Aviation Consumer Protection Division has jurisdiction over charters and provides a certain degree of protection. The DOT requires that money paid to charter operators be held in escrow, so if you can't pay with a credit card, **always make your check payable to a charter carrier's escrow account.** The name of the bank should be in the charter contract. If you have any problems with a charter operator, contact the DOT (☞ Airline Complaints, *below*). If you buy a charter package that includes both air and land arrangements, remember that the escrow requirement applies only to the air component.

CONSOLIDATORS

Consolidators buy tickets for scheduled international flights at reduced rates from the airlines, then sell them at prices that beat the best fare available directly from the airlines, usually without restrictions. Sometimes you can even get your money back if you need to return the ticket. Carefully read the fine print detailing penalties for changes and cancellations, and **confirm your consolidator reservation with the airline.**

➤ CONSOLIDATORS: **Cheap Tickets** (☎ 800/377–1000). **Up & Away Travel** (☎ 212/889–2345). **Discount Travel Network** (☎ 800/576–1600). **Unitravel** (☎ 800/325–2222). **World Travel Network** (☎ 800/409–6753).

COURIERS

When you fly as a courier, you trade your checked-luggage space for a ticket subsidized by a courier service. It's all perfectly legitimate, but there are restrictions: You can usually book your flight only a week or two in advance, your length of stay may be set for a certain number of days, and you probably won't be able to book a companion on the same flight.

CUTTING COSTS

The least-expensive airfares to Munich are priced for round-trip travel and usually must be purchased in advance. It's smart to **call a number of airlines, and when you are quoted a good price, book it on the spot**—the same fare may not be available the next day. Airlines generally allow you to change your return date for a fee. If you don't use your ticket, you can apply the cost toward the purchase of a new ticket, again for a small charge. However, most low-fare tickets are nonrefundable. To get the lowest airfare, **check different routings.** Compare prices of flights to and from different airports if your destination or home city has more than one gateway. Also price off-peak flights, which may be significantly less expensive.

Travel agents, especially those who specialize in finding the lowest fares (☞ Discounts & Deals, *below*), can be especially helpful when booking a plane ticket. When you're quoted a price, **ask your agent if the price is likely to get any lower.** Good agents know the seasonal fluctuations of airfares and can usually anticipate a sale or fare war. However, waiting can be risky: The fare could go *up* as seats become scarce, or you may wait so long that your preferred flight sells out. A wait-and-see strategy works best if your plans are flexible. If you must arrive and depart on certain dates, don't delay.

CHECK IN & BOARDING
Airlines routinely overbook planes, assuming that not everyone with a ticket will show up, but sometimes everyone does. When that happens, airlines ask for volunteers to give up their seats. In return these volunteers usually get a certificate for a free flight and are rebooked on the next flight out. If there are not enough volunteers, the airline must choose who will be denied boarding. The first to get bumped

are passengers who checked in late and those flying on discounted tickets, so **get to the gate and check in as early as possible,** especially during peak periods.

Although the trend on international flights is to drop reconfirmation requirements, many airlines still ask you to reconfirm each leg of your international itinerary. Failure to do so may result in your reservation being canceled.

Always **bring a government-issued photo ID to the airport.** You may be asked to show it before you are allowed to check in.

ENJOYING THE FLIGHT
For more legroom, **request an emergency-aisle seat.** Don't sit in the row in front of the emergency aisle or in front of a bulkhead, where seats may not recline.

If you don't like airline food, **ask for special meals when booking.** These can be vegetarian, low-cholesterol, or kosher, for example.

When flying internationally, try to maintain a normal routine, to help fight jet-lag. At night, **get some sleep.** By day, **eat light meals, drink water (not alcohol), and move around the cabin** to stretch your legs.

Many carriers have prohibited smoking on all of their international flights; others allow smoking only on certain routes or certain departures, so **contact your carrier regarding its smoking policy.**

HOW TO COMPLAIN

If your baggage goes astray or your flight goes awry, complain right away. Most carriers require that you **file a claim immediately.**

➤ AIRLINE COMPLAINTS: U.S. Department of Transportation **Aviation Consumer Protection Division** (✉ C-75, Room 4107, Washington, DC 20590, ☎ 202/366–2220). **Federal Aviation Administration Consumer Hotline** (☎ 800/322–7873).

AIRPORT

Franz Josef Strauss (FJS) Airport (☎ 011–49–89/97500), named after the late Bavarian state premier, is 28 km (17 mi) northeast of the city center, between the small towns of Freising and Erding.

TRANSFERS TO DOWNTOWN

By Bus: The bus service to the city is slower and more expensive (DM 15) than the S-bahn link (☞ Public Transportation, *below*) and is not recommended.

By Car: From the airport to the city, take route A–9 and follow the signs for München Stadtmitte. From the city to the airport, head north through Schwabing, join the A–9 Autobahn at the Frankfurter Ring intersection, and follow the signs for the airport (FLUGHAFEN).

By Taxi: The taxi fare from the airport costs between DM 90 and DM 100. During rush hour (7 AM–10 AM and 4 PM–7 PM) allow up to one hour of traveling time.

By Train: A fast train service links FJS Airport with Munich's Hauptbahnhof (the main train station). The S-8 line operates from a terminal directly beneath the airport's arrival and departure halls. Trains leave every 20 minutes, and the journey takes 38 minutes. Several intermediate stops are made, including Ostbahnhof (convenient for lodgings east of the Isar River) and city-center stations like Marienplatz. A one-way ticket costs DM 13.20, DM 10.40 if you purchase a multiple-use "strip" ticket (☞ Public Transportation, *below*). A family of up to five (two adults and three children) can make the trip for DM 24 by buying a *Tageskarte* ticket.

BIKING

Munich and its environs are easily navigated on two wheels. The city is threaded with a network of specially designated bike paths. A free map showing all bike trails is available at all city tourist offices. A list of S-bahn and mainline stations that offer the service is also available from the Deutsche Bahn. The cost is DM 6–DM 8 a day if you've used public transportation to reach the station; otherwise it's DM 10–DM 12, depending on the type of bike. ☞ Walking and Biking *in* Guided Tours, *below*.

➤ BIKE RENTALS: **Englischer Garten** (✉ Königstr. and Veterinärstr., ☎ 089/397–016); DM 5 per hour or DM 15 for the day from May through October, weekends in good weather. **Aktiv-Rad** (⊠ Hans-Sachs Str. 7, ☎ 089/266–506). **Hauptbahnhof** (⊠ Radius Touristik, opposite platform 31, ☎ 089/596113); April through October.

BUS TRAVEL

Long-distance buses arrive at and depart from the north side of the main train station. A taxi stand is right next to it.

BUSINESS HOURS

BANKS

Banks are generally open weekdays from 8:30 or 9 to 2 or 3 (5 or 6 on Thursday), with a lunch break of about an hour. Branches at airports and main train stations open as early as 6:30 AM and close as late as 10:30 PM.

MUSEUMS

Most museums are open from Tuesday to Sunday 9–6. Some close for an hour or more at lunch, and some are open on Monday. Many stay open late on Wednesday or Thursday.

SHOPS

Department stores and larger shops are generally open 9 or 9:15–8PM weekdays and until 4 PM on Saturday. If you plan to shop in a department store try to do it in the morning or early afternoon, as Munich department stores report that 15% of their business is now done between 6:30 and 8 PM.

CAMERAS & COMPUTERS

EQUIPMENT PRECAUTIONS

Always **keep your film, tape, or computer disks out of the sun.** Carry an extra supply of batteries, and **be prepared to turn on your camera, camcorder, or laptop** to prove to security personnel that the device is real. Always **ask for hand inspection of film,** which becomes clouded after successive exposure to airport X-ray machines, and **keep videotapes and computer disks away from metal detectors.**

CAR RENTAL

Rates with the major car rental companies begin at about $18 per day and $100 per week for an economy car with air-conditioning, a manual transmission, and unlimited mileage. This does not include tax on car rentals, which is 16%.

➤ MAJOR AGENCIES: **Avis** (☎ 800/331–1084, 800/879–2847 in Canada, 008/225–533 in Australia). **Budget** (☎ 800/527–0700, 0800/181181 in the U.K.). **Hertz** (☎ 800/654–3001, 800/263–0600 in Canada, 0345/555888 in the U.K., 03/9222–2523 in Australia, 03/358–6777 in New Zealand). **National InterRent** (☎ 800/227–3876; 0345/222525 in the U.K., where it is known as Europcar InterRent).

➤ WITHIN MUNICH: **Avis** (⊠ Nymphenburgerstr. 61, ☎ 089/1260–0020; ⊠ Balanstr. 74,

☎ 089/403–091). **Europcar** (✉ Hirtenstr. 14, ☎ 089/ 557–145). **Hertz** (✉ Nymphen-burgerstr. 81, ☎ 089/129–5001). **Sixt-Budget** (✉ Seitzstr. 9, ☎ 089/ 223–333).

CUTTING COSTS

To get the best deal, **book through a travel agent who is willing to shop around.**

Also **ask your travel agent about a company's customer-service record.** How has the company responded to late plane arrivals and vehicle mishaps? Are there often lines at the rental counter? If you're traveling during a holiday period, does a confirmed reservation guarantee you a car?

Be sure to **look into wholesalers,** companies that do not own fleets but rent in bulk from those that do and often offer better rates than traditional car-rental operations. Prices are best during off-peak periods. Rentals booked through wholesalers must be paid for before you leave the United States.

➤ RENTAL WHOLESALERS: **Auto Europe** (☎ 207/842–2000 or 800/ 223–5555, FAX 800/235–6321). **Europe by Car** (☎ 212/581–3040 or 800/223–1516, FAX 212/246–1458). **DER Travel Services** (✉ 9501 W. Devon Ave., Rosemont, IL 60018, ☎ 800/782–2424, FAX 800/282–7474 for information or 800/860–9944 for brochures). **Kemwel Holiday Autos** (☎ 914/ 835–5555 or 800/678–0678, FAX 914/835–5126).

INSURANCE

When driving a rented car you are generally responsible for any damage to or loss of the vehicle. Collision policies that car-rental companies sell for European rentals typically do not cover stolen vehicles. Before you buy additional insurance, **see what coverage you already have** under the terms of your personal auto-insurance policy and credit cards—you may already be covered.

REQUIREMENTS

In Germany your own driver's license is acceptable, but an International Driver's Permit is a good idea; it's available from the American or Canadian automobile association, and, in the United Kingdom, from the Automobile Association or Royal Automobile Club. These international permits are universally recognized, and having one in your wallet may save you a problem with the local authorities.

SURCHARGES

Before you pick up a car in one city and leave it in another, **ask about drop-off charges or one-way service fees,** which can be substantial. Note, too, that some rental agencies charge extra if you return the car before the time specified in your contract. To avoid a hefty refueling fee, **fill the**

tank just before you turn in the car, but be aware that gas stations near the rental outlet may overcharge.

CAR TRAVEL

Entry formalities for motorists are few: All you need is proof of insurance, an international car-registration document, and a U.S. or Canadian driver's license (an international license is helpful, but not a must). If you or your car are from an EU country, Norway, or Switzerland, all you need is your domestic license and proof of insurance. *All* foreign cars must have a country sticker.

To reach Munich from the north (Nürnberg or Frankfurt), leave the autobahn at the Schwabing exit. From Stuttgart and the west, the autobahn ends at Obermenzing. The autobahns from Salzburg and the east, Garmisch and the south, and Lindau and the southwest all join the Mittlerer Ring (city beltway). When leaving any autobahn, follow the Stadtmitte signs for downtown Munich.

AUTO CLUBS

➤ IN MUNICH: Two of the three principal automobile clubs in Germany are in Munich: **ADAC** (Allgemeiner Deutscher Automobil-Club, ⊠ Am Westpark 8, D–81373, ☎ 089/76760), and **DTC** (Deutscher Touring-Automobil Club, ⊠ Amalienburgstr. 23, D–81247, ☎ 089/891–1330).

➤ IN AUSTRALIA: **Australian Automobile Association** (☎ 06/247–7311).

➤ IN CANADA: **Canadian Automobile Association** (CAA, ☎ 613/247–0117).

➤ IN NEW ZEALAND: **New Zealand Automobile Association** (☎ 09/377–4660).

➤ IN THE U.K.: **Automobile Association** (AA, ☎ 0990/500–600), **Royal Automobile Club** (RAC, ☎ 0990/722–722 for membership, 0345/121–345 for insurance).

➤ IN THE U.S.: **American Automobile Association** (☎ 800/564–6222).

EMERGENCY SERVICES

ADAC (☞ Auto Clubs, *above*) operates tow trucks on all autobahns; emergency telephones are every 3 km (2 mi). On minor roads, **go to the nearest call box and dial 01802/222–222.** Ask, in English, for road service assistance. Help is free (with the exception of all materials) if the work is carried out by the ADAC. If the ADAC has to use a subcontactor for the work, charges are made for time, mileage, and materials.

GASOLINE

Gasoline (petrol) costs are between DM 1.20 and DM 1.70 per liter. As part of antipollution efforts, most German cars now run on lead-free fuel and leaded gas is becoming more and more difficult to find. Some models use diesel fuel, so if you are renting a car, **find out which fuel the car takes.** Some older vehicles cannot take unleaded fuel. German filling stations are highly competitive and bargains are often available if you shop around, but *not* at autobahn filling stations. Self-service, or *SB-Tanken,* stations are cheapest. Pumps marked *Bleifrei* contain unleaded gas.

RULES OF THE ROAD

In Germany you drive on the right, and road signs give distances in kilometers. There is no speed limit on autobahns, although drivers are advised to keep below 130 km (80 mi) per hour. Speed limits on non-autobahn country roads vary from 80 to 100 km (50 to 60 mi) per hour. Alcohol limits on drivers are equivalent to two small beers or a quarter of a liter of wine. Note that seat belts must be worn at all times by front- *and* back-seat passengers.

CHILDREN & TRAVEL

CHILDREN IN MUNICH

Munich's tourist offices (☞ Visitor Information, *below*) have booklets of information recommending ways to entertain children in the city, including listings of children's theaters, puppet theaters, and movie houses. Playgrounds seem to pop up every several blocks.

If you are renting a car don't forget to **arrange for a car seat** when you reserve. Most hotels in Germany allow children under a certain age to stay in their parents' room at no extra charge, but others charge them as extra adults; be sure to **ask about the cutoff age for children's discounts.**

➤ BABY-SITTING: For recommended local sitters, **check with your hotel desk.** Updated lists of well-screened baby-sitters are also available from most local tourist offices. Rates are usually about DM 25 per hour. Many large department stores in Germany provide baby-sitting facilities or areas where children can play while their parents shop.

FLYING

If your children are two or older, **ask about children's airfares.** As a general rule, infants under two not occupying a seat fly at greatly reduced fares or even for free.

In general the adult baggage allowance applies to children paying half or more of the adult fare. When booking, **ask about carry-on allowances for those traveling with infants.** In general, for babies charged 10% of the adult fare you are allowed one carry-on bag and a collapsible stroller, which may have to be checked; you may be limited to less if the flight is full.

Experts agree that it's a good idea to use safety seats aloft for children weighing less than 40 pounds. Airlines, however, can set their own policies: U.S. carriers allow FAA-approved models but usually require that you buy a ticket, even if your child would otherwise ride free, since the seats must be strapped into regular seats. Airline rules vary, so it's important to **check your airline's policy about using safety seats during takeoff and landing.** Safety seats cannot obstruct the movement of other passengers in the row, so get an appropriate seat assignment as early as possible.

When making your reservation, **request children's meals or a free-standing bassinet** if you need them; the latter are available only to those seated at the bulkhead, where there's enough legroom. Remember, however, that bulkhead seats may not have their own overhead bins, and there's no storage space in front of you—a major inconvenience.

CONSULATES

U.S. Consulate General, ⊠ Königinstr. 5, ☎ 089/28880. **British Consulate General,** ⊠ Bürkleinstr. 10, ☎ 089/211–090. **Canadian Consulate,** ⊠ Tal 29, ☎ 089/290–650.

CONSUMER PROTECTION

Whenever possible, **pay with a major credit card** so you can cancel payment or get reimbursed if there's a problem, provided that you can show documentation. This is the best way to pay, whether you're buying travel arrangements before your trip or shopping at your destination.

If you're doing business with a particular company for the first time, **contact your local Better Business Bureau and the attorney general's offices** in your state and the company's home state, as well. Have any complaints been filed?

Finally, if you're buying a package or tour, always **consider travel insurance** that includes default coverage (☞ Insurance, *below*).

➤ LOCAL BBBs: **Council of Better Business Bureaus** (⊠ 4200 Wilson Blvd., Suite 800, Arlington, VA 22203, ☎ 703/276–0100, ℻ 703/525–8277).

CUSTOMS & DUTIES

When shopping, **keep receipts** for all of your purchases. Upon reentering the country, **be ready to show customs officials what you've bought.** If you feel a duty is incorrect, appeal the assessment. If you object to the way your clearance was handled, get the inspector's badge number. In either case, first ask to see a supervisor, then write to the appropriate authorities, beginning with the port director at your point of entry.

IN GERMANY

Since a single, unrestricted market took effect within the European Union (EU) early in 1993, there are no longer restrictions for citizens of the 15 member countries traveling between EU countries.

For instance, travelers may import 800 cigarettes, 120 bottles of wine, and 10 liters of alcohol, provided the goods have been bought duty-paid, i.e., not in a duty-free shop. For citizens of non-EU countries and anyone entering Germany from outside the Union, the following limitations apply.

On goods obtained anywhere outside the EU or for goods purchased in a duty-free shop within an EU country, you are allowed (1) 200 cigarettes or 100 cigarillos or 50 cigars or 250 grams of tobacco (twice that if you live outside of Europe); (2) 2 liters of still table wine; (3) 1 liter of spirits over 22% volume or 2 liters of spirits under 22% volume (fortified and sparkling wines) or 2 more liters of table wine; (4) 60 milliliters of perfume and 250 milliliters of toilet water; (5) other goods to the value of DM 115.

Tobacco and alcohol allowances are for visitors age 17 and over. Other items intended for personal use can be imported and exported freely. There are no restrictions on the import and export of German currency.

IN AUSTRALIA

Australia residents who are 18 or older may bring back $A400 worth of souvenirs and gifts (including jewelry), 250 cigarettes or 250 grams of tobacco, and 1,125 ml of alcohol (including wine, beer, and spirits). Residents under 18 may bring back $A200 worth of goods.

➤ INFORMATION: **Australian Customs Service** (Regional Director, ✉ Box 8, Sydney, NSW 2001, ☎ 02/9213–2000, FAX 02/9213–4000).

IN CANADA

Canadian residents who have been out of Canada for at least seven days may bring in C$500 worth of goods duty-free. If you've been away less than seven days but more than 48 hours, the duty-free allowance drops to C$200; if your trip lasts 24–48 hours, the allowance is C$50. You may not pool allowances with family members. Goods claimed under the C$500 exemption may follow you by mail; those claimed under the lesser exemptions must accompany you. Alcohol and tobacco products may be included in the seven-day and 48-hour exemptions but not in the 24-hour exemption. If you meet the age requirements of the province or territory through which you reenter Canada, you may bring in, duty-free, 1.14 liters (40 imperial ounces) of wine or liquor or 24 12-ounce cans or bottles of beer or ale. If you are 16 or older you may bring in, duty-free, 200 cigarettes and 50 cigars.

You may send an unlimited number of gifts worth up to C$60 each duty-free to Canada. Label the package UNSOLICITED GIFT—VALUE UNDER $60. Alcohol and tobacco are excluded.

➤ INFORMATION: **Revenue Canada** (✉ 2265 St. Laurent Blvd. S, Ottawa, Ontario K1G 4K3, ☎ 613/993–0534, 800/461–9999 in Canada).

IN NEW ZEALAND

Homeward-bound residents with goods to declare must present themselves for inspection. If you're 17 or older, you may bring back $700 worth of souvenirs and gifts. Your duty-free allowance also includes 4.5 liters of wine or beer; one 1,125-ml bottle of spirits; and either 200 cigarettes, 250 grams of tobacco, 50 cigars, or a combo of all three up to 250 grams.

➤ INFORMATION: **New Zealand Customs** (✉ Custom House, ✉ 50 Anzac Ave., Box 29, Auckland, New Zealand, ☎ 09/359–6655, ☎ 09/309–2978).

IN THE U.K.

If you are a U.K. resident and your journey was wholly within the European Union (EU), you won't have to pass through customs when you return to the United Kingdom. If you plan to bring back large quantities of alcohol or tobacco, check EU limits beforehand.

➤ INFORMATION: **HM Customs and Excise** (✉ Dorset House, ✉ Stamford St., London SE1 9NG, ☎ 0171/202–4227).

IN THE U.S.

U.S. residents may bring home $400 worth of foreign goods duty-free if they've been out of the country for at least 48 hours (and if they haven't used the $400 allowance or any part of it in the past 30 days).

U.S. residents 21 and older may bring back 1 liter of alcohol duty-free. In addition, regardless of your age, you are allowed 200 cigarettes and 100 non-Cuban cigars. Antiques, which the U.S. Customs Service defines as objects more than 100 years old, enter duty-free, as do original works of art done entirely by hand, including paintings, drawings, and sculptures.

You may also send packages home duty-free: up to $200 worth of goods for personal use, with a limit of one parcel per addressee per day (and no alcohol or tobacco products or perfume worth more than $5); label the package PERSONAL USE, and attach a list of its contents and their retail value. Do not label the package UNSOLICITED GIFT, or your duty-free exemption will drop to $100. Mailed items do not affect your duty-free allowance on your return.

➤ INFORMATION: **U.S. Customs Service** (Inquiries, ✉ Box 7407, Washington, DC 20044, ☎ 202/927–6724; complaints, Office of Regulations and Rulings, ✉ 1301 Constitution Ave. NW, Washington, DC 20229; registration of equipment, Resource Management, ✉ 1301 Constitution Ave. NW, Washington DC 20229, ☎ 202/927–0540).

DISABILITIES & ACCESSIBILITY

ACCESS IN GERMANY

Nearly 100 German cities and towns issue special guides for visitors with disabilities, which offer information, usually in German, about how to get around destinations and suggestions for places to visit.

All the major hotel chains (Hilton, Sheraton, Marriott, Holiday Inn, Steigenberger, and Kempinski) have special facilities for guests with disabilities, including specially equipped and furnished rooms. Some leading privately owned hotels also cater to travelers with disabilities; local tourist offices can provide lists of these hotels and additional information.

MAKING RESERVATIONS

When discussing accessibility with an operator or reservations agent, **ask hard questions.** Are there any stairs, inside *or* out? Are there grab bars next to the toilet *and* in the shower/tub? How wide is the doorway to the room? To the bathroom? For the most extensive facilities meeting the latest legal specifications, **opt for newer accommodations,** which are more likely to have been designed with access in mind. Older buildings or ships may have more limited facil-

ities. Be sure to **discuss your needs before booking.**

TRAIN TRAVEL

The Deutsche Bahn (German Rail) provides a complete range of services and facilities for travelers with disabilities. All InterCity Express (ICE) and InterRegio trains and most EuroCity and InterCity trains have special areas for wheelchair users. Seat and wheelchair-space reservations are free of charge for wheelchair users. The German Red Cross and a welfare service called the Bahnhofs-Mission (Railway Station Mission) have support facilities at all major and many smaller, regional stations. They organize assistance in boarding, leaving, and changing trains and also help with reservations.

Deutsche Bahn issues a booklet detailing its services for travelers with disabilities, with an English-language section. It can be obtained from **Deutsche Bahn AG** (German Rail, ✉ Stephensonstr. 1 D–60326 Frankfurt am Main, ☎ 069/97330). Assistance can also be obtained from individual railroad stations by calling the local number 19419 (without the town or city prefix). Most railroad stations have English-speaking staff handling information inquiries.

➤ COMPLAINTS: **Disability Rights Section** (✉ U.S. Department of Justice, Civil Rights Division, ✉

Box 66738, Washington, DC 20035–6738, ☎ 202/514–0301 or 800/514–0301, TTY 202/514–0383 or 800/514–0383, 🕾 202/307–1198) for general complaints. **Aviation Consumer Protection Division** (☞ Air Travel, *above*) for airline-related problems. **Civil Rights Office** (⊠ U.S. Department of Transportation, Departmental Office of Civil Rights, S-30, ⊠ 400 7th St. SW, Room 10215, Washington, DC, 20590, ☎ 202/366–4648, 🕾 202/366–9371) for problems with surface transportation.

TRAVEL AGENCIES & TOUR OPERATORS

As a whole, the travel industry has become more aware of the needs of travelers with disabilities. In the U.S., the Americans with Disabilities Act requires that travel firms serve the needs of all travelers. Note, though, that some agencies and operators specialize in making travel arrangements for individuals and groups with disabilities.

➤ TRAVELERS WITH MOBILITY PROBLEMS: **Access Adventures** (⊠ 206 Chestnut Ridge Rd., Rochester, NY 14624, ☎ 716/889–9096), run by a former physical-rehabilitation counselor. **Accessible Journeys** (⊠ 35 W. Sellers Ave., Ridley Park, PA 19078, ☎ 610/521–0339 or 800/846–4537, 🕾 610/521–6959), for escorted tours exclusively for travelers with mobility impairments. **CareVacations** (⊠ 5019 49th Ave., Suite 102, Leduc, Alberta T9E

6T5, ☎ 403/986–6404, 800/648–1116 in Canada) has group tours and is especially helpful with cruise vacations. **Flying Wheels Travel** (⊠ 143 W. Bridge St., Box 382, Owatonna, MN 55060, ☎ 507/451–5005 or 800/535–6790, 🕾 507/451–1685), a travel agency specializing in customized tours and itineraries worldwide. **Hinsdale Travel Service** (⊠ 201 E. Ogden Ave., Suite 100, Hinsdale, IL 60521, ☎ 630/325–1335), a travel agency that benefits from the advice of wheelchair traveler Janice Perkins.

DISCOUNTS & DEALS

Be a smart shopper and **compare all your options** before making any choice. A plane ticket bought with a promotional coupon may not be cheaper than the least expensive fare from a discount ticket agency. For high-price travel purchases, such as packages or tours, keep in mind that what you get is just as important as what you save. Just because something is cheap doesn't mean it's a bargain.

CLUBS & COUPONS

Many companies sell discounts in the form of travel clubs and coupon books, but these cost money. You must use participating advertisers to get a deal, and only after you recoup the initial membership cost or book price do you begin to save. If you plan to use the club or coupons frequently, you may save considerably. Before signing up, find out what discounts you get for free.

➤ DISCOUNT CLUBS: **Entertainment Travel Editions** (✉ 2125 Butterfield Rd., Troy, MI 48084, ☎ 800/445–4137; $20–$51, depending on destination). **Great American Traveler** (✉ Box 27965, Salt Lake City, UT 84127, ☎ 801/974–3033 or 800/548–2812; $49.95 per year). **Moment's Notice Discount Travel Club** (✉ 7301 New Utrecht Ave., Brooklyn, NY 11204, ☎ 718/234–6295; $25 per year, single or family). **Privilege Card International** (✉ 237 E. Front St., Youngstown, OH 44503, ☎ 330/746–5211 or 800/236–9732; $74.95 per year). **Sears's Mature Outlook** (✉ Box 9390, Des Moines, IA 50306, ☎ 800/336–6330; $19.95 per year). **Travelers Advantage** (✉ CUC Travel Service, ✉ 3033 S. Parker Rd., Suite 1000, Aurora, CO 80014, ☎ 800/548–1116 or 800/648–4037; $59.95 per year, single or family). **Worldwide Discount Travel Club** (✉ 1674 Meridian Ave., Miami Beach, FL 33139, ☎ 305/534–2082; $50 per year family, $40 single).

CREDIT-CARD BENEFITS

When you use your credit card to make travel purchases you may get free travel-accident insurance, collision-damage insurance, and medical or legal assistance, depending on the card and the bank that issued it. American Express, MasterCard, and Visa provide one or more of these services, so **get a copy of your credit card's travel-benefits policy.** If you are a member of an auto club, always **ask hotel and car-rental reservations agents about auto-club discounts.** Some clubs offer additional discounts on tours, cruises, and admission to attractions.

DISCOUNT RESERVATIONS

To save money, **look into discount-reservations services** with toll-free numbers, which use their buying power to get a better price on hotels, airline tickets, even car rentals. When booking a room, always **call the hotel's local toll-free number** (if one is available) rather than the central reservations number— you'll often get a better price. Always ask about special packages or corporate rates.

When shopping for the best deal on hotels and car rentals, **look for guaranteed exchange rates,** which protect you against a falling dollar. With your rate locked in, you won't pay more, even if the price goes up in the local currency.

➤ AIRLINE TICKETS: ☎ **800/FLY–4–LESS.**

➤ HOTEL ROOMS: **Hotels Plus** (☎ 800/235–0909). **International Marketing & Travel Concepts** (☎ 800/790–4682). **Steigenberger Reservation Service** (☎ 800/223–5652). **Travel Interlink** (☎ 800/888–5898).

ELECTRICITY

To use your U.S.-purchased electric-powered equipment, **bring a converter and adapter.** The electrical current in Germany is 220 volts, 50 cycles alternating current (AC); wall outlets take continental-type plugs, with two round prongs.

If your appliances are dual-voltage, you'll need only an adapter. Don't use 110-volt outlets, marked FOR SHAVERS ONLY, for high-wattage appliances such as blow-dryers. Most laptops operate equally well on 110 and 220 volts and so require only an adapter.

EMERGENCIES

➤ CONTACTS: **Police:** ☎ 089/110. **Fire department:** ☎ 089/112. **Ambulance:** ☎ 089/19222. **Medical emergencies:** ☎ 089/557–755. **Pharmacy service:** ☎ 089/594–475.

GAY & LESBIAN TRAVEL

➤ GAY- AND LESBIAN-FRIENDLY TRAVEL AGENCIES: **Corniche Travel** (✉ 8721 Sunset Blvd., Suite 200, West Hollywood, CA 90069, ☎ 310/854–6000 or 800/429–8747, FAX 310/659–7441). **Islanders Kennedy Travel** (✉ 183 W. 10th St., New York, NY 10014, ☎ 212/242–3222 or 800/988–1181, FAX 212/929–8530). **Now Voyager** (✉ 4406 18th St., San Francisco, CA 94114, ☎ 415/626–1169 or 800/255–6951, FAX 415/626–8626). **Yellowbrick Road** (✉ 1500 W. Balmoral Ave., Chicago, IL 60640, ☎ 773/561–1800 or 800/642–2488, FAX 773/561–4497). **Skylink Travel and Tour** (✉ 3577 Moorland Ave., Santa Rosa, CA 95407, ☎ 707/585–8355 or 800/225–5759, FAX 707/584–5637), serving lesbian travelers.

GUIDED TOURS

EXCURSIONS

The S-bahn can quickly take you to some of the most beautiful places in the countryside around Munich. Line S-6, for example, will whisk you lakeside to Starnbergersee in a half hour; Line S-4 runs to the depths of the Ebersberger Forest. You can take a bicycle on S-bahn trains.

Bus excursions to the Alps, to Austria, to the royal palaces and castles of Bavaria, or along the Romantic Road can be booked through **ABR** (✉ Hauptbahnhof, ☎ 089/591–315 or 089/59041). **Panorama Tours** (✉ Arnulfstr. 8, next to the Hauptbahnhof, ☎ 089/591–504) operates numerous trips, including the Royal Castles Tour (Schlösserfahrt) of "Mad" King Ludwig's dream palaces; the cost is DM 75, excluding entrance fees to the palaces. Bookings can also be made through all major hotels in the city. The tours depart from in front of the Hauptbahnhof outside the Hertie department store.

ORIENTATION

A variety of city bus tours is offered by **Panorama Tours** (✉ Arnulfstr. 8, ☎ 089/591–504). The blue buses operate year-round, departing from in front of the Hertie department store on Bahnhofplatz (⊠ across from the main entrance to the train station). The Kleine Rundfahrt, a one-hour city tour, leaves daily at 10 AM and 2:30 PM, as well as 11:30 AM and 4 PM in midsummer. The cost is DM 15. The Olympiatour, which lasts about 2½ hours, explores the Olympia Tower and grounds; it departs daily at 10 AM and 2:30 PM, and the cost is DM 27. The Grosse Rundfahrt, or extended city tour, comes in two varieties; each lasts around 2½ hours and costs DM 27. The morning tour includes visits to the Frauenkirche and Residenz; the afternoon tour visits Schloss Nymphenburg. They run Tuesday–Sunday, leaving at 10 and 2:30, respectively. One 2½-hour city tour includes a visit to the Bavaria Film Studios. It leaves at 10 AM and costs DM 35. The München bei Nacht tour provides 4½ hours of Munich by night and includes dinner and a show at the Hofbräuhaus, a trip up the Olympic Tower to admire the lights of the city, and a final drink in a nightclub. It departs May–October, Friday and Saturday at 7:30 PM; the cost is DM 100.

WALKING & BICYCLING
The Munich tourist office (☞ Visitor Information, *below*) organizes guided walking tours for groups or individuals; no advance booking is necessary. The meeting place is the Fischbrunnen (Fish Fountain) on Marienplatz on Monday, Tuesday, and Thursday at 10 AM; the cost is DM 6 per person. **Münchner Stadtrundgänge** has a daily tour, starting at 9:30 AM at the Mariensäule in the middle of Marienplatz. The tour costs DM 10. Call Siegfried Sturm ☎ 089/181–273 to book.

➤ BIKE TOURS: **City Hopper Touren** (☎ 089/272–1131) offers daily escorted bike tours March–October. Bookings must be made in advance, and starting times are negotiable. **Radius Touristik** (⊠ Arnulfstr. 3, opposite platforms 30–36 in the Hauptbahnhof main concourse, ☎ 089/596–113) has bicycle tours from May through the beginning of October at 10:15 and 2; the cost, including bike rental, is DM 15. **Mike's Bike Tours** (☎ 089/651–4275) is run by a young American who hires German students to take visitors on a two- to three-hour spin through Munich. The tours start daily at the Old Town Hall, the Altes Rathaus, at 11:20 and 3:50. They cost DM 28, including bike rental.

HEALTH

DOCTORS AND DENTISTS
The American, British, and Canadian Consulate Generals (☞ *above*) have lists of recommended doctors and dentists who speak English.

MEDICAL PLANS

No one plans to get sick while traveling, but it happens, so **consider signing up with a medical-assistance company.** Members get doctor referrals, emergency evacuation or repatriation, 24-hour telephone hotlines for medical consultation, cash for emergencies, and other personal and legal assistance. Coverage varies by plan, so **review the benefits of each carefully.**

➤ MEDICAL-ASSISTANCE COMPANIES: **International SOS Assistance** (⊠ 8 Neshaminy Interplex, Suite 207, Trevose, PA 19053, ☎ 215/245–4707 or 800/523–6586, FAX 215/244–9617; ⊠ 12 Chemin Riantbosson, 1217 Meyrin 1, Geneva, Switzerland, ☎ 4122/785–6464, FAX 4122/785–6424; ⊠ 10 Anson Rd., 14-07/08 International Plaza, Singapore, 079903, ☎ 65/226–3936, FAX 65/226–3937).

PHARMACIES

Munich pharmacies stay open late on a rotating basis, and every pharmacy has a sign in its window with the address of the nearest drug store that's open late.

➤ LOCATIONS: **Internationale Ludwigs-Apotheke** (⊠ Neuhauserstr. 11, ☎ 089/260–3021), open weekdays 8–6 and Saturday 8–1, and **Europa-Apotheke** (⊠ Schützenstr. 12, near the Hauptbahnhof, ☎ 089/595–423), open weekdays 8–6 and Saturday 8–1, stock a large variety of over-the-counter medications and personal-hygiene products.

HIKING

➤ TRAIL INFORMATION: **Deutscher Alpenverein** (⊠ Von-Kahr-Str. 2–4, D–80997 Munich, ☎ 089/140–030) has information on Alpine walking. It maintains more than 50 mountain huts and about 15,000 km (9,300 mi) of Alpine paths. In addition, it can provide courses in mountaineering and touring suggestions for routes in both winter and summer. Foreigners may become members. Various mountaineering schools offer weeklong courses ranging from basic techniques for beginners to advanced mountaineering. Tourist offices in all Bavarian Alpine resorts have details.

HOLIDAYS

The following national holidays are observed in Munich: January 1; January 6 (Epiphany); April 2 (Good Friday); April 5 (Easter Monday); May 1 (Workers' Day); May 13 (Ascension); May 24 (Pentecost Monday); June 3 (Corpus Christi); August 15 (Assumption Day); October 3 (German Unity Day); November 1 (All Saints' Day); December 24–26 (Christmas).

INSURANCE

Travel insurance is the best way to **protect yourself against financial loss.** The most useful plan is a comprehensive policy that includes coverage for trip cancellation and interruption, default, trip delay, and medical expenses (with a waiver for preexisting conditions).

Without insurance, you will lose all or most of your money if you cancel your trip, regardless of the reason. Default insurance covers you if your tour operator, airline, or cruise line goes out of business. Trip-delay covers unforeseen expenses that you may incur due to bad weather or mechanical delays. It's important to compare the fine print regarding trip-delay coverage when comparing policies.

For overseas travel, one of the most important components of travel insurance is its medical coverage. Supplemental health insurance will pick up the cost of your medical bills should you get sick or injured while traveling. U.S. residents should note that Medicare generally does not cover health-care costs outside the United States, nor do many privately issued policies. Residents of the United Kingdom can buy an annual travel-insurance policy valid for most vacations taken during the year in which the coverage is purchased. If you are pregnant or have a pre-existing condition, make sure you're covered. British citizens should buy extra medical coverage when traveling overseas, according to the Association of British Insurers. Australian travelers should

buy travel insurance, including extra medical coverage, whenever they go abroad, according to the Insurance Council of Australia.

Always **buy travel insurance directly from the insurance company**; if you buy it from a cruise line, airline, or tour operator that goes out of business you probably will not be covered for the agency or operator's default. Before you make any purchase, **review your existing health and home-owner's policies** to find out whether they cover expenses incurred while traveling.

➤ TRAVEL INSURERS: In the U.S., **Access America** (✉ 6600 W. Broad St., Richmond, VA 23230, ☎ 804/285–3300 or 800/284–8300). **Travel Guard International** (✉ 1145 Clark St., Stevens Point, WI 54481, ☎ 715/345–0505 or 800/826–1300). In Canada, **Mutual of Omaha** (✉ Travel Division, ✉ 500 University Ave., Toronto, Ontario M5G 1V8, ☎ 416/598–4083, 800/268–8825 in Canada).

➤ INSURANCE INFORMATION: In the U.K., **Association of British Insurers** (✉ 51 Gresham St., London EC2V 7HQ, ☎ 0171/600–3333). In Australia, the **Insurance Council of Australia** (☎ 613/9614–1077, FAX 613/9614–7924).

LANGUAGE

The Germans are great linguists and you'll find that English is spoken in virtually all hotels, restaurants, airports, stations, museums, and other places of interest.

Unless you speak fluent German, you may find the regional dialect of Bavaria hard to follow. Most Germans can speak "High," or standard, German, and can switch modes if they see you are having trouble understanding them.

LODGING

The standard of German hotels—from sophisticated luxury spots (of which the country has more than its fair share) to the humblest country inn—is very high. Rates vary enormously, though not disproportionately, in comparison with other northern European countries. You can nearly always **expect courteous and polite service and clean and comfortable rooms.** Larger hotels often have no-smoking rooms or even no-smoking floors, so it's always worth asking for one when you check in.

Lists of German hotels are available from the German National Tourist Office and all regional and local tourist offices. (Most hotels have restaurants, but those listed as *Garni* will provide breakfast only.) Tourist offices will also make bookings for you at a nominal fee, but they may have difficulty doing so after 4 PM in high season and on weekends, so **don't wait until too late in the day to begin looking for your accommodations.** (If you do get stuck, ask someone who looks like a native—a mail carrier, police officer, or waiter, for example—for directions to a house renting *Fremdenzimmer,* meaning simply "rooms" in a private house.

Note that there is no official nationwide grading system for hotels in Germany, although some regional tourist authorities operate their own. Rates are by no means inflexible, and depend very much on supply and demand; you can save money by inquiring about reductions. Some hotels in the city cut their prices on weekends and when business is quiet. Always **be careful about trying to book late in the day at peak times.** If you have booked and plan to arrive late, let the hotel know. And if you have to cancel a reservation, let the hotel know as soon as possible, otherwise you may be charged the full amount for the unused room. During trade fairs (most commonly held in the spring and fall), rates in city hotels can rise appreciably. Breakfast is usually, but not always, included. Inexpensive rooms may not have a shower or tub. **Ask about breakfast and bathing facilities** when booking. When you arrive, if you don't like the room you're offered, ask to see another.

➤ RESERVATIONS: An excellent nationwide hotel reservation service is also operated by **Turistische Informations-und Buchungssysteme (TIBS,** ✉ Freiburg im Breisgau, ☎ 0761/885–810, 🖷 0761/885–

8129), open weekdays 9–6 and Saturday 9–1. The service is free of charge.

HOSTELS

You can save on lodging costs by staying at a hostel. In Bavaria however, **there is an age limit of 27.** Germany's youth hostels—*Jugendherbergen* —are probably the most efficient, up-to-date, and proportionally numerous of any country's. Preference is also given to members of a national youth hosteling or Hostelling International (HI); nonmembers pay an extra DM 6–DM 7 for the first six nights' accommodation, after which normal hostel charges are levied. These range from about DM 15 to DM 21 (breakfast included). Cards are available from the American Youth Hostels Association, the Canadian Hostelling Association, and the United Kingdom's Youth Hostels Association.

➤ HOSTEL ORGANIZATIONS: **Hostelling International—American Youth Hostels** (✉ 733 15th St. NW, Suite 840, Washington, DC 20005, ☎ 202/783–6161, FAX 202/783–6171). **Hostelling International—Canada** (✉ 400-205 Catherine St., Ottawa, Ontario K2P 1C3, ☎ 613/237–7884, FAX 613/237–7868). **Youth Hostel Association of England and Wales** (✉ Trevelyan House, 8 St. Stephen's Hill, St. Albans, Hertfordshire AL1 2DY, ☎ 01727/855215 or 01727/845047, FAX 01727/844126); membership in

the U.S. \$25, in Canada C\$26.75, in the U.K. £9.30).

➤ IN GERMANY: **Deutsches Jugendherbergswerk Hauptverband** (✉ Postfach 1455, D–32704 Detmold, ☎ 05231/74010) has listings of German youth hostels.

MAIL

POSTAL RATES

Airmail letters to the United States and Canada cost DM 3; postcards cost DM 2. All letters to the United Kingdom cost DM 1.10; postcards cost DM 1.

RECEIVING MAIL

You can arrange to have mail sent to you in care of any German post office; **have the envelope marked "Postlagernd."** This service is free. Alternatively, have mail sent to any American Express office in Germany. There's no charge to cardholders, holders of American Express traveler's checks, or anyone who has booked a vacation with American Express.

MONEY

CREDIT & DEBIT CARDS

Should you use a credit card or a debit card when traveling? Both have benefits. A credit card allows you to delay payment and gives you certain rights as a consumer (☞ Consumer Protection, *above*). A debit card, also known as a check card, deducts funds directly from your checking account and helps you stay within your budget. If you want to rent a car, though, you may still need an old-fashioned credit card. Although you can always *pay* for your car with a debit card, some agencies will not allow you to *reserve* a car with a debit card.

Otherwise, the two types of plastic are virtually the same. Both will get you cash advances at ATMs worldwide if your card is properly programmed with your personal identification number (PIN). (For use in Germany, your PIN must be four digits long.) Both offer excellent wholesale exchange rates. And both protect you against unauthorized use if the card is lost or stolen. Your liability is limited to $50, as long as you report the card missing.

➤ ATM LOCATIONS: **Cirrus** (☎ 800/424–7787). **Plus** (☎ 800/843–7587) for locations in the U.S. and Canada, or visit your local bank.

CURRENCY

The European Union currency unit, the Euro, makes its official appearance on January 1, 1999, although it will take two years for the complete introduction of the new banknotes and coins. Deutschmarks will still be the official currency for everyday use in 1999, although some shops might begin to price their wares in Euros. Don't let that confuse you, and continue to think in terms of Deutschmarks—at least until the year 2002, when full currency union takes effect. The

Deutschmark (DM) is divided into 100 pfennigs (pf). There are bills of 5 (rare), 10, 20, 50, 100, 200, 500, and 1,000 marks and coins of 1, 2, 5, 10, and 50 pfennigs and 1, 2, and 5 marks. At press time, the mark stood at DM 1.79 to the U.S. dollar, DM 1.20 to the Canadian dollar, and DM 2.98 to the pound sterling.

EXCHANGING MONEY

For the most favorable rates, **change money through banks.** Although fees charged for ATM transactions may be higher abroad than at home, Cirrus and Plus exchange rates are excellent, because they are based on wholesale rates offered only by major banks. You won't do as well at exchange booths in airports or rail and bus stations, in hotels, in restaurants, or in stores, although you may find their hours more convenient. To avoid lines at airport exchange booths, **get a bit of local currency before you leave home.**

➤ EXCHANGE SERVICES: **Chase Currency To Go** (☎ 800/935–9935; 935–9935 in NY, NJ, and CT). **International Currency Express** (☎ 888/842–0880 on the East Coast, 888/278–6628 on the West Coast). **Thomas Cook Currency Services** (☎ 800/287–7362 for telephone orders and retail locations).

TRAVELER'S CHECKS

Lost or stolen checks can usually be replaced within 24 hours. To ensure a speedy refund, buy your own traveler's checks—don't let someone else pay for them. Likewise, the person who bought the checks should make the call to request a refund.

PACKING

LUGGAGE

How many carry-on bags you can bring with you is up to the airline. Most allow two, but on certain flights the limit is often reduced to one. Gate agents will take excess baggage—including bags they deem oversize—from you as you board and add it to checked luggage. To avoid this situation, make sure that everything you carry aboard will fit under your seat. Also, get to the gate early, and request a seat at the back of the plane; you'll probably board first, while the overhead bins are still empty. Since big, bulky baggage attracts the attention of gate agents and flight attendants on a busy flight, make sure your carry-on is really a carry-on. Finally, a carry-on that's long and narrow is more likely to remain unnoticed than one that's wide and squarish.

Before departure, **itemize your bags' contents** and their worth, and label the bags with your name, address, and phone number. (If you use your home address, cover it so that potential thieves can't see it readily.) Inside each bag, **pack a copy of your itinerary.** At check-in, **make sure that each** bag is correctly tagged** with the destination airport's three-letter code. If your bags arrive damaged or fail to arrive at all, file a written report with the airline before leaving the airport.

PACKING LIST

What you pack depends more on the time of year than on any particular dress code. Winters can be bitterly cold; summers are warm but with days that suddenly turn cool and rainy. In summer **take a warm jacket or heavy sweater** for the Bavarian Alps, where the nights can be chilly even after hot days.

Pack as you would for an American city: dressy outfits for formal restaurants and nightclubs, casual clothes elsewhere. Jeans are as popular in Germany as anywhere else and are perfectly acceptable for sightseeing and informal dining. In the evening, men will probably feel more comfortable wearing a jacket and tie in more expensive restaurants, although it is almost never required. Many German women are extremely fashion-conscious and wear stylish outfits to restaurants and the theater, especially in the larger cities.

To discourage purse snatchers and pickpockets, **carry a handbag with long straps** that you can sling across your body, bandolier-style, and a zippered compartment for money and other valuables.

For stays in budget hotels, **take your own soap.** Many provide no soap at all or only one small bar.

In your carry-on luggage **bring an extra pair of eyeglasses or contact lenses** and **enough of any medication you take** to last the entire trip. You may also want your doctor to write a spare prescription using the drug's generic name, since brand names may vary from country to country. **Never put prescription drugs or valuables in luggage to be checked.** To avoid customs delays, carry medications in their original packaging. And don't forget to copy down and carry addresses of offices that handle refunds of lost traveler's checks.

PASSPORTS & VISAS
When traveling internationally, **carry a passport even if you don't need one** (it's always the best form of I.D.), and make **two photocopies of the data page** (one for someone at home and another for you, carried separately from your passport). If you lose your passport, promptly call the nearest embassy or consulate and the local police.

ENTERING GERMANY
U.S., Canadian, and British citizens need only a valid passport to enter Germany for stays of up to 90 days.

PASSPORT OFFICES
The best time to apply for a passport or to renew is during the fall and winter. Before any trip, be sure to check your passport's expiration date and, if necessary, renew it as soon as possible. (Some countries won't allow you to enter on a passport that's due to expire in six months or less.)

➤ AUSTRALIAN CITIZENS: **Australian Passport Office** (☎ 131–232).

➤ CANADIAN CITIZENS: **Passport Office** (☎ 819/994–3500 or 800/567–6868).

➤ NEW ZEALAND CITIZENS: **New Zealand Passport Office** (☎ 04/494–0700 for information on how to apply, 0800/727–776 for information on applications already submitted).

➤ U.K. CITIZENS: **London Passport Office** (☎ 0990/21010), for fees and documentation requirements and to request an emergency passport.

➤ U.S. CITIZENS: **National Passport Information Center** (☎ 900/225–5674; calls are charged at 35¢ per minute for automated service, $1.05 per minute for operator service).

PUBLIC TRANSPORTATION
Munich has an efficient and well-integrated public transportation system, consisting of the **U-bahn** (subway), the **S-bahn** (suburban railway), the **Strassenbahn** (streetcars), and buses. Marienplatz forms the heart of the U-bahn and S-bahn network, which operates from around 5 AM to 1 AM. An all-night tram and bus service oper-

ates on main routes within the city. For a clear explanation in English of how the system works, pick up a copy of *Rendezvous mit München,* available free of charge at all tourist offices.

FARES

Fares are uniform for the entire public transportation system. As long as you are traveling in the same direction, you can transfer from one mode of transportation to another on the same ticket. You can also interrupt your journey as often as you like, and time-punched tickets are valid for up to four hours, depending on the number of zones you travel through. Fares are constantly creeping upwards, but at press time a basic **Einzelfahrkarte** (one-way ticket) costs DM 3.40 for a ride in the inner zone and DM 1.70 for a short journey of up to four stops. If you plan to take a number of trips around the city, you'll save money by buying a **Mehrfahrtenkarte,** or multiple strip ticket. Red strip tickets are valid for children under 15 only. Blue strips cover adults. DM 15 buys an 11-strip ticket. All but the shortest inner-area journeys (up to four stops) cost two strips, which must be canceled at one of the many time-punching machines at stations or on buses and trams. For a short stay the simplest idea is the **Tageskarte** ticket, which provides unlimited travel for up to five people (maximum of two adults, plus three children under 15). It is valid weekdays from 9 AM to 4 AM the following day and at any time on weekends. The costs are DM 12 for an inner-zone ticket and DM 24 for the entire network.

All tickets can be purchased from the blue dispensers at U- and S-bahn stations and at bus and streetcar stops. Bus and streetcar drivers, all tourist offices, and Mehrfahrtenkarten booths (which display a white *K* on a green background) also sell tickets. Spot checks are common and carry an automatic fine of DM 60 if you're caught without a valid ticket. One final tip: Holders of a EurailPass, a Youth Pass, an Inter-Rail card, or a Deutsche Bahn Tourist Card can travel free on all S-bahn trains.

SENIOR-CITIZEN TRAVEL

In Germany, the number of citizens over 60 is growing; this section of the population has also become more affluent and even has its own political party, the Gray Panthers. The strength of this special-interest age group has won them special privileges in Germany—such as price adjustments on the railways and reduced admission to museums—and older visitors from abroad can also take advantage of these discounts. Contact the German National Tourist Office (☞ Visitor Information, *below*).

To qualify for age-related discounts, **mention your senior-citizen status up front** when booking hotel reservations (not when checking out) and before you're seated in restaurants (not when paying the bill). Note that discounts may be limited to certain menus, days, or hours. When renting a car, **ask about promotional car-rental discounts,** which can be cheaper than senior-citizen rates.

➤ EDUCATIONAL PROGRAMS: **Elderhostel** (✉ 75 Federal St., 3rd floor, Boston, MA 02110, ☎ 617/426–8056). **Interhostel** (✉ University of New Hampshire, 6 Garrison Ave., Durham, NH 03824, ☎ 603/862–1147 or 800/733–9753, ℻ 603/862–1113).

STUDENT TRAVEL

HOSTELING
☞ Lodging, *above.*

TRAVEL AGENCIES
To save money, **look into deals available through student-oriented travel agencies.** To qualify you'll need a bona fide student I.D. card. Members of international student groups are also eligible.

➤ STUDENT I.D.s & SERVICES: **Council on International Educational Exchange** (✉ CIEE, 205 E. 42nd St., 14th floor, New York, NY 10017, ☎ 212/822–2600 or 888/268–6245, ℻ 212/822–2699), for mail orders only, in the United States. **Travel Cuts** (✉ 187 College St., Toronto, Ontario M5T 1P7, ☎ 416/979–2406 or 800/667–2887) in Canada.

➤ STUDENT TOURS: **Contiki Holidays** (✉ 300 Plaza Alicante, Suite 900, Garden Grove, CA 92840, ☎ 714/740–0808 or 800/266–8454, ℻ 714/740–2034).

TAXIS
Munich's cream-color taxis are numerous. Hail them in the street or call 089/21610 (there's an extra charge of DM 2 for the drive to the pickup point). Rates start at DM 4. There is an additional charge of DM 1 for each piece of luggage. Expect to pay DM 12–DM 13 for a short trip within the city.

TELEPHONES

COUNTRY CODES
The country code for Germany is 49. When dialing a German number from abroad, drop the initial 0 from the local area code.

DIRECTORY & OPERATOR INFORMATION
The German telephone system is fully automatic, and it's unlikely that you'll have to employ the services of an operator, unless you're seeking information. If you have difficulty reaching your number or want to book a reverse-charge call, dial 010, or 0010 for international calls. For information, dial 11833. International operators speak English, and English-speaking staff are close at hand for other services.

INTERNATIONAL CALLS

International calls can be made from public phones bearing the sign INLANDS UND AUSLANDSGE-SPRÄCHE. Using DM 5 coins is best for long-distance dialing; a four-minute call to the United States costs DM 15. To avoid weighing yourself down with coins, however, use a phone card or **make international calls from post offices**; even those in small country towns will have a special booth for international calls. You pay the clerk the cost of the call, plus a DM 2 connection fee. Never make international calls from your hotel room; rates will be at least double the regular charge.

AT&T, MCI, and Sprint international access codes make calling the United States relatively convenient, but you may find the local access number blocked in many hotel rooms. First ask the hotel operator to connect you. If the hotel operator balks, ask for an international operator, or dial the international operator yourself. One way to improve your odds of getting connected to your long-distance carrier is to travel with more than one company's calling card (a hotel may block Sprint, for example, but not MCI). If all else fails, call from a pay phone in the hotel lobby.

➤ ACCESS CODES: **AT&T Direct** (☎ 800/435–0812). **MCI World-Phone** (☎ 800/444–4141). **Sprint International Access** (☎ 800/877–4646).

PUBLIC PHONES

Local public phones charge a minimum 30 pfennigs per call (for six minutes). All public phones take 10 pf, DM 1, and DM 5 coins, although coin-operated call boxes are rapidly giving way to card-operated ones. So you're advised to **buy a phone card,** particularly if you're anticipating making a lot of phone calls. You can purchase a phone card at any German post office (also available at many exchange places). They come in denominations of DM 12 and DM 50, the latter good for DM 60 worth of calls. Most phone booths have instructions in English as well as German.

TIPPING

The service charges on bills suffice for most tips in your hotel, though you should **tip bellhops and porters**; DM 2 per bag or service is ample. It's also customary to leave a small tip (a couple of marks per night) for the room cleaning staff. Whether you tip the desk clerk depends on whether he or she has given you any special service.

Service charges are included in all restaurant checks (listed as *Bedienung*), as is tax (listed as *MWST*). Nonetheless, it is customary to **round up the bill to the nearest mark or to leave about 5%** (give it to the waiter or waitress as you pay the bill; don't leave it on the table).

In taxis, **round up the fare to the nearest full mark** as a tip. Only give more if you have particularly cumbersome or heavy luggage (though you will be charged 50 pfennigs for each piece of luggage anyway).

TOUR OPERATORS

Buying a prepackaged tour or independent vacation can make your trip to Germany less expensive and more hassle-free. Because everything is prearranged, you'll spend less time planning.

Operators that handle several hundred thousand travelers per year can use their purchasing power to give you a good price. Their high volume may also indicate financial stability. But some small companies provide more personalized service; because they tend to specialize, they may also be more knowledgeable about a given area.

BOOKING WITH AN AGENT

Travel agents are excellent resources. In fact, large operators accept bookings made only through travel agents. But it's a good idea to **collect brochures from several agencies,** because some agents' suggestions may be influenced by relationships with tour and package firms that reward them for volume sales. If you have a special interest, **find an agent with expertise in that area**; ASTA (☞ Travel Agencies, *below*) has a database of specialists worldwide.

Make sure your travel agent knows the accommodations and other services. You may want to ask about the hotel's location, room size, beds, and whether it has a pool, room service, or programs for children. Has your agent been there in person or sent others you can contact?

Do some homework on your own, too: Local tourism boards can provide information about lesser-known and small-niche operators, some of which may sell only direct.

BUYER BEWARE

Each year consumers are stranded or lose their money when tour operators—even very large ones with excellent reputations—go out of business. So **check out the operator.** Find out how long the company has been in business, and ask several travel agents about its reputation. If the package or tour you are considering is priced lower than in your wildest dreams, **be skeptical.** Try to **book with a company that has a consumer-protection program.** If the operator has such a program, you'll find information about it in the company's brochure. If the operator you are considering does not offer some kind of consumer protection, then ask for references from satisfied customers.

In the U.S., members of the National Tour Association and United States Tour Operators Association are required to set aside funds to cover your payments and travel arrangements in case the company defaults. It's also a good idea to choose a company that participates in the American Society of Travel Agent's Tour Operator Program (TOP). This gives you a forum if there are any disputes between you and your tour operator; ASTA will act as mediator.

➤ TOUR-OPERATOR RECOMMENDATIONS: **American Society of Travel Agents** (☞ Travel Agencies, *below*). **National Tour Association** (✉ NTA, 546 E. Main St., Lexington, KY 40508, ☎ 606/226–4444 or 800/755–8687). **United States Tour Operators Association** (✉ USTOA, 342 Madison Ave., Suite 1522, New York, NY 10173, ☎ 212/599–6599 or 800/468–7862, FAX 212/599–6744).

COSTS

The more your package or tour includes, the better you can predict the ultimate cost of your vacation. Make sure you know exactly what is covered, and **beware of hidden costs.** Are taxes, tips, and service charges included? Transfers and baggage handling? Entertainment and excursions? These can add up.

Prices for packages and tours are usually quoted per person, based on two sharing a room. If traveling solo, you may be required to pay the full double-occupancy rate. Some operators eliminate this surcharge if you agree to be matched with a roommate of the same sex, even if one is not found by departure time.

PACKAGES

Independent vacation packages are available from major tour operators and airlines. The companies listed below offer vacation packages in a broad price range.

➤ AIR/HOTEL: **Delta Vacations** (☎ 800/872–7786). **DER Tours** (✉ 9501 W. Devon St., Rosemont, IL 60018, ☎ 800/937–1235, FAX 847/692–4141 or 800/282–7474, 800/860–9944 for brochures). **TWA Getaway Vacations** (☞ Group Tours, *above*). **US Airways Vacations** (☎ 800/455–0123).

➤ FROM THE U.K.: **DER Travel Services Ltd.** (✉ 18 Conduit St., London W1R 9TD, ☎ 0171/290–0111) arranges self-catering, guest-house, and hotel vacations. The **German Travel Centre** (✉ 403–409 Rayner's La., Pinner, Middlesex, HA5 5ER, ☎ 0181/429–2900) arranges tailor-made vacations. **Moswin Tours Ltd.** (✉ 21 Church St., Oadby, Leicester LE2 5DB, ☎ 0116/271–9922) specializes in spa resorts and city breaks in Germany.

TRAIN TRAVEL

All long-distance rail services arrive at and depart from Munich's Hauptbahnhof, the main train station; trains to and from some destinations in Bavaria use the adjoining Starnbergerbahnhof, which is under the same roof as the Hauptbahnhof. The high-speed InterCity Express trains connect Munich, Frankfurt, and Hamburg on one line; Munich, Würzburg, and Hamburg on another. For information on train schedules, call 089/19419; most railroad information staff speak English. For tickets, reservations and travel information, go to the station information office or try the ABR travel agency, right by the station on Bahnhofplatz.

TRAVEL AGENCIES

A good travel agent puts your needs first. Look for an agency that has been in business at least five years, emphasizes customer service, and has someone on staff who specializes in your destination. In addition, **make sure the agency belongs to a professional trade organization,** such as ASTA in the United States. If your travel agency is also acting as your tour operator, *see* Buyer Beware in Tour Operators, *above*).

➤ LOCAL AGENT REFERRALS: **American Society of Travel Agents** (ASTA, ☎ 800/965–2782 24-hr hotline, FAX 703/684–8319). **Association of Canadian Travel Agents** (✉ 1729 Bank St., Suite 201, Ottawa, Ontario K1V 7Z5, ☎ 613/521–0474, FAX 613/521–0805). **Association of British Travel Agents** (✉ 55–57 Newman St., London W1P 4AH, ☎ 0171/637–2444, FAX 0171/637–0713). Aus-tralian Federation of Travel Agents (☎ 02/9264–3299). **Travel Agents' Association of New Zealand** (☎ 04/499–0104).

➤ WITHIN MUNICH: **American Express,** ✉ Promenadepl. 6, ☎ 089/290–900. **ABR,** ☎ 089/12040 the official Bavarian travel agency, has outlets all over Munich.

VISITOR INFORMATION

Munich Found, an English-language monthly, has articles and information about the city, as well as a complete calendar of events. It's sold (DM 4) in kiosks downtown. The *Monatsprogramm,* an official monthly listing of upcoming events, is available at most hotels and newsstands and all tourist offices for DM 2.50.

➤ BAVARIAN MOUNTAIN REGION: **Tourismusverband München-Oberbayern** (Upper Bavarian Regional Tourist Office, ✉ Bodenseestr. 113, D-81243, ☎ 089/829–1802).

➤ GERMAN NATIONAL TOURIST OFFICE: **U.S. Nationwide:** (✉ 122 E. 42nd St., New York, NY 10168, ☎ 212/661–7200, FAX 212/661–7174). **Canada:** (✉ 175 Bloor St. E, Suite 604, Toronto, Ontario M4W 3R8, ☎ 416/968–1570, FAX 416/968–1986). **U.K.:** (✉ Nightingale House, 65 Curzon St., London W1Y 8NE, ☎ 0171/493–0081 or 0891/600–100 for brochures, FAX 0171/495–6129). Calls to the brochure line cost 50p per minute peak rate, 45p at all other times.

➤ Munich Tourist Offices: The **airport tourist office** (☎ 089/9759-2815) is open Monday–Saturday 8:30 AM–10 PM and Sunday 1–9. The **Fremdenverkehrsamt** (central tourist office) is in the heart of the city (⊠ Rindermarkt 10, just up the street from central Marienpl., ☎ 089/23911), open Monday–Thursday 8:30–4 and Friday 8:30–2). Longer hours are kept by the city tourist office at the **Hauptbahnhof** train station (⊠ Bahnhofpl. 2, next to the ABR travel agency, ☎ 089/233-30256 or 089/233-30257), open Monday–Saturday 10–8 and Sunday 10–6, and by the **Info-Service** (⊠ Marienplatz, ☎ 089/089/233-30272 or 089/233-30273) within the Rathaus building, open weekdays 10–8, Saturday 10–4.

WHEN TO GO

WEATHER

Germany's climate is temperate, although cold spells can make the thermometer plunge well below freezing, particularly in the Bavarian Alps to the south of Munich. Summers are usually sunny and warm, though you should **be prepared for a few cloudy and wet days.** The south is normally always a few degrees warmer than the north. As you get nearer to the Alps, however, the summers get shorter, often not beginning until the end of May. Fall is sometimes spectacular in the south—warm and soothing. The only real exception is the strikingly variable weather in South Bavaria caused by the *Föhn,* an Alpine wind that gives rise to clear but very warm conditions. The Föhn can occur in all seasons. Sudden atmospheric pressure changes associated with the Föhn give some people headaches.

The following are the average daily maximum and minimum temperatures for Munich.

Climate in Munich

Jan.	35F	1C	May	64F	18C	Sept.	67F	20C
	23	− 5		45	7		48	9
Feb.	38F	3C	June	70F	21C	Oct.	56F	14C
	23	− 5		51	11		40	4
Mar.	48F	9C	July	74F	23C	Nov.	44F	7C
	30	− 1		55	13		33	0
Apr.	56F	14C	Aug.	73F	23C	Dec.	36F	2C
	38	3		54	12		26	− 4

1 Destination: Munich

WELCOME TO MUNICH

MUNICH—München to the Germans—third-largest city in the Federal Republic and capital of the Free State of Bavaria, is the single most popular tourist destination for Germans. This one statistic attests to the enduring appeal of what by any standard is a supremely likable city. Munich is kitsch and class, vulgarity and elegance. It's a city of ravishing rococo and smoky beer cellars, of soaring Gothic and sparkling shops, of pale stucco buildings and space-age factories, of millionaires and lederhosen-clad farmers. Germany's favorite city is a place with extraordinary ambience and a vibrant lifestyle all its own, in a splendid setting within view—on a clear day—of the towering Alps.

Munich belongs to the relaxed and sunny south. Call it Germany with a southern exposure—although it may be an exaggeration to claim, as some Bavarians do, that Munich is the only Italian city north of the Alps. Still, there's no mistaking the carefree spirit that infuses the city, and its easygoing approach to life, liberty, and the pursuit of happiness, Bavarian style. The Bavarians refer to this

positively un-Teutonic joie de vivre as Gemütlichkeit.

What makes Munich so special? One explanation is the flair for the fanciful that is deeply rooted in Bavarian culture. And no historical figure better personifies this tradition than Ludwig II, one of the last of the Wittelsbachs, the royal dynasty that for almost 750 years ruled over Munich and southern Germany, until the monarchy was forced to abdicate in 1918. While Bismarck was striving from his Berlin power base to create a modern unified Germany, "Mad" Ludwig—also nicknamed the "Dream King"—was almost bankrupting the state's treasury by building a succession of fairy-tale castles and remote summer retreats in the mountains and countryside.

Munich bills itself as *Die Weltstadt mit Herz* (the cosmopolitan city with heart), which it most assuredly is. A survey suggests that most Germans would prefer to live in Munich than where they currently reside, even though it is probably the most expensive place in reunited Germany. This is not to suggest that all Germans subscribe to the "I Love Munich" concept. Certain buttoned-up types—in Hamburg or Düsseldorf, for example—might look down their imperious noses at Munich as just a mite crass and somewhat tacky, and Bavarians as only a few rungs up from the barbarians. So be it.

Munich's stock image is the cavernous beer hall (such as the world-famous Hofbräuhaus) filled with the deafening echo of a brass oompah band and rows of swaying, burly Bavarians in lederhosen being served by frumpy Fraus in flaring dirndl dresses. Every day in different parts of the city, you'll find scenes like this. But there are also many Müncheners who never step inside a beer hall, who never go near Oktoberfest. They belong to the *other* Munich: a city of charm, refinement, and sophistication, represented by two of the world's most important art galleries and a noted opera house; a city of expensive elegance, where high-fashion shops seem in competition to put the highest price tags on their wares; a city of five-star nouvelle cuisine.

Endowed with vast, green tracts of parks, gardens, and forests; grand boulevards set with remarkable edifices; fountains and statuary; and a river spanned by graceful bridges, Munich is easily Germany's most beautiful and interesting city. If the traveler could visit only one city in Germany, this should be it—no question. If you factor in the city's dramatic change over the past decade, a

traveler who has not visited for awhile might find a whole new Munich has evolved in the interim. For, quietly and without fanfare, Munich has taken its place as the high-tech capital of Germany, developing into the number-one postindustrial-age center in the country and one of the most important cities in Europe. The concentration of electronics and computer firms—Siemens, IBM, Apple, and the like—in and around the city has turned it into the Silicon Valley of Germany.

PLEASURES AND PASTIMES

Beer and Beer Gardens

Munich has more than 100 beer gardens, ranging from huge establishments that seat several hundred guests to small terraces tucked behind neighborhood pubs and taverns. Beer gardens are such an integral part of Munich life that a council proposal to cut down their hours provoked a storm of protest in 1995, culminating in one of the largest mass demonstrations in the city's history. They open whenever the thermometer creeps above 10°C (42°F) or so and when the sun filters through the chestnut trees that are a necessary part of the beer-garden scenery. Most—but not all—allow you to bring along your own food, and if you do, try not to bring something so foreign as pizza or a burger from McDonald's.

BEER GLOSSARY➤ The alcohol content of German beers varies considerably. At the weaker end of the scale is the light Munich Helles (3.7% alcohol by volume); stronger brews are Pilsner (around 5%) and Doppelbock (more than 7%).

Bock: strong beer, which can be light or dark, sweet or dry.

Doppelbock: stronger than Bock, usually dark, and not to be trifled with.

Dunkles: dark beer, often slightly sweeter or maltier than pale (light) beers.

Export: usually a pale (light-colored) beer of medium strength.

Halbe: half a Mass, the standard beer measure in Bavaria (☞ *below*).

Hefe: yeast.

Helles: light beer.

Klar, Kristall: wheat beer with the yeast removed.

Kleines: a small glass of beer (in Bavaria).

Lager: literally, "store"; that stage of the brewing process when beer matures in the brewery.

Leichtbier: beer with low alcohol and calorie content, usually pale in color.

Mass: a 1-liter (almost 2-pint) glass or earthenware mug.

Naturtrüb: a new term for unfiltered beer, implying the yeast has not been removed.

Obergärig: top-fermented.

Pils, Pilsner: a golden-color, dry, bitter-flavored beer named after Pilsen, the Czech town where in the 19th century the brewing style was first developed.

Polizei Stunde: literally, "police hour"—closing time; midnight or 1 AM in some big cities, usually earlier in small towns and villages.

Prost: German for "cheers."

Radler: lemonade and beer mixed.

Rauchbier: smoked beer; usually a dark brew with a smoky flavor that comes from infusing the malted barley with beech-wood smoke.

Untergärig: bottom-fermented.

Weissbier, Weizenbier: wheat beer; a highly carbonated, sharp, and sour brew, often with floating yeast particles.

Dining

Old Munich restaurants, called *Gaststätten,* feature *gutbürgerliche Küche,* loosely translated as good regional fare, and include brewery restaurants, beer halls, beer gardens, rustic cellar establishments, and *Weinstüben* (wine taverns).

Munich is also a great place for snacks. The city's pre–McDonald's-type fast food is a centuries-old tradition. A tempting array of delectables is available almost anytime day or night; knowing the various Bavarian names will help. The generic term for Munich snacks is *Schmankerl*. And Schmankerl are served at *Brotzeit,* literally translated as "bread time": a snack break, or what the English might call elevenses. According to a saying, *"Brotzeit ist die schönste Zeit"* (snack time is the best time).

In the morning in Munich, one eats *Weisswurst,* a tender minced-veal sausage—made fresh daily, steamed, and served with sweet mustard, a crisp roll or a pretzel, and *Weissbier* (wheat beer). This white sausage is not to everyone's taste, but it is certainly worth trying. As legend has it, this sausage was invented in 1857 by a butcher who had a hangover and mixed the wrong ingredients. A plaque on a wall in Marienplatz marks where the "mistake" was made. It is claimed the genuine article is available only in and around Munich and served only between midnight and noon.

Another favorite Bavarian specialty is *Leberkäs*—literally "liver cheese," although neither liver nor cheese is involved in its construction. It is a spicy meat loaf baked to a crusty turn each morning and served in succulent slabs throughout the day. A *Leberkäs Semmel*—a wedge of the meat loaf between two halves of a crispy bread roll smeared with a bittersweet mustard—is the favorite Munich on-the-hoof snack.

After that comes the repertoire of sausages indigenous to Bavaria, including types from Regensburg and Nürnberg.

More substantial repasts include *Tellerfleisch,* boiled beef with freshly grated horseradish and boiled potatoes on the side, served on wooden plates. (There is a similar dish called *Tafelspitz.*)

Among roasts, *Sauerbraten* (beef) and *Schweinebraten* (pork) are accompanied by dumplings and red cabbage or sauerkraut.

Haxn (ham hocks) are roasted until they're crisp on the outside, juicy on the inside. They are served with sauerkraut and potato puree.

You'll also find soups, salads, fish and fowl, cutlets, game in season, casseroles, hearty stews, desserts, and what may well be the greatest variety and the highest quality of baked goods in Europe, including pretzels. In particular, seek out a *Käsestange*—a crispy long bread roll coated in baked cheese. No one need ever go hungry or thirsty in Munich.

Music and Opera

Munich and music complement each other marvelously. The city has two world-renowned orchestras (one, the Philharmonic, is now directed by the American conductor James Levine), the Bavarian State Opera Company, wonderful choral ensembles, two opera houses (the chief of these, the Bavarian State Opera, is managed by an ingenious British director, Peter Jonas), a rococo jewel of a court theater, and a modern Philharmonic concert hall of superb proportions and acoustics—and that's just for starters.

Shopping

Munich has three of Germany's most exclusive shopping streets. At the other end of the scale, it has a variety of flea markets to rival that of any other European city. In between are department stores, where acute German-style competition assures reasonable prices and often produces outstanding bargains. The Christmas markets, which spring up all over the city as November slides into December, draw from backroom-studio artisans and artists with wares of outstanding beauty and originality. Collect their business cards—in the summer you're sure to want to order another of those little gold baubles that were on sale in December.

QUICK TOURS

If you're here for just a short period you need to plan carefully so as to make the most of your time in Munich. The following itineraries outline major sights throughout the city and will help you structure your visit efficiently. Each is intended to take about four hours—a perfect way to fill a free morning or afternoon. For more information about individual sights, *see* Chapter 2.

Tour 1

Start this central Munich tour on Marienplatz square shortly before 11 AM, when the elaborate Glockenspiel (carillon) in the tower of the neo-Gothic Neues Rathaus (city hall) clanks into action. There's a tourist-information office in the Rathaus. The city's original city hall, the Altes Rathaus, is on the eastern edge of the square; you can admire it only from outside. Exit Marienplatz on the south, along the old cattle market, Rindermarkt, and get a bird's-eye view of the city from the tower of St. Peter's Church. The city's central market, the Viktualienmarkt, is south of St. Peter's, and you can sample Munich beer and meat specialties at one of the many market stalls. Stroll down Rosental to Sendlingerstrasse for the one must-see Munich church interior: the ornate 18th-century Asamkirche. Explore the jumble of streets behind the church, and within five minutes you'll be in the city's shopping mile, the Neuhauser-Kaufinger-Strasse mall. Head east toward Marienplatz, your starting and ending point, but leave time for a visit to the city's cathedral, the Frauenkirche. Its brick towers signal the way.

Tour 2

Marienplatz is again the starting point. Duck under the arches of the former city hall, the Altes Rathaus, turn left into Burgstrasse, and you'll find a peaceful square lined by medieval buildings that were once the site of the original Wittelsbach royal palace, the Alter Hof. Its successor, the Residenz, is a few hundred yards north. Cross Maximilianstrasse and Max-Josef-Platz (the opera house on your right) to reach it. Exploring the Residenz (closed Monday) will take a couple of hours; afterwards stroll north to the royal gardens, the Hofgarten. On the way, look at the Feldherrnhalle (an imitation Florentine loggia abused as a Nazi shrine) and the Baroque Theatinerkirche. Finish your tour with coffee at Munich's oldest cafe, the Tambosi, on Odeonsplatz.

Tour 3

This museum tour starts at the main railway station, the Hauptbahnhof, where there is a tourist-information office. Head northwest, through the original botanical gardens, the Alter Botanischer Garten, and continue up Meiserstrasse to Königsplatz. If antiquities are your thing, visit the two fine museums of Greek, Etruscan, and Roman art on either side of the huge square (the Antikensammlungen and the Glyptothek). For something more modern, continue up Meiserstrasse, which turns into Arcisstrasse, and on the right you'll find the Alte Pinakothek and Neue Pinakothek, Munich's leading art galleries. Visit museums in the afternoon, when school groups have passed through, and end your tour at happy hour in one of the many bars and cafés in this part of Schwabing, the old artists' quarter.

Tour 4

Don walking shoes for this tour through Munich's huge city park, the Englischer Garten. The starting point is Odeonsplatz (U3 and U6 subway stop), which leads into the old royal gardens, the Hofgarten, and thence into the Englischer Garten. On the right as you cross into the park you'll see one of the few remnants of Nazi architecture in Munich—the Haus der Kunst, a major art gallery and home to Munich's top disco, the PI. Return there after dark, if that's your scene, but first introduce yourself to Munich beer at the city's most celebrated beer garden, the Chinesischer Turm (Chinese Tower), named after the replica of a Chinese pagoda that stands incongruously in the midst of leafy English-style parkland. Work up a thirst again with a 1-km walk north to the park's largest stretch of water, the Kleinhesselohesee, where you'll find a more upmarket beer garden. Walk around the lake and head south to Odeonsplatz, trying to synchronize this part of your tour with the sunset behind Munich's steepled panorama.

2 Exploring Munich

CHIC AND COSMOPOLITAN, carefree and kitschy—as Bavaria's capital and one of Germany's biggest cities, Munich has more than its share of great museums, architectural treasures, historic sites, and world-class shops, restaurants, and hotels. The same could be said of its abundance of lederhosen and oompah bands. But it's the overall feeling of *Gemütlichkeit* (conviviality) that makes the city so special—an open-air market here, a park there, and beer halls everywhere. Tourists flock to Munich year-round, but festival dates—especially *Fasching,* or Carnival, in the winter, and *Oktoberfest* in the fall—draw the most.

Munich is one of Europe's wealthiest cities—and it shows. Here everything is extremely upscale and up-to-date. At times the aura of affluence may be all but overpowering. But that's what Munich is all about these days and nights: a new city superimposed on the old; conspicuous consumption on a scale we can hardly imagine as a way of life; a fresh patina of glitter along with the traditional rustic charms. Such are the dynamics and duality of this fascinating metropolis that remains a joy to explore and get to know.

Numbers in the text correspond to numbers in the margin and on the Munich map.

The City Center

Munich is unique among German cities because it has no identifiable, homogeneous Old Town center. The historic heart of the city is a quiet courtyard unknown to most tourists, while clusters of centuries-old buildings that belong to Munich's origins are often separated by postwar developments of sometimes singular ugliness. The outer perimeter of this tour is defined more by a visitor's stamina than by ancient city walls.

A Good Walk

Begin your walk through the city center at the **Hauptbahnhof** ①, the main train station and site of the city tourist office, which is next to the station's main entrance, on Bahnhofplatz. Pick up a detailed city map here. Cross Bahnhofplatz, the square in front of the station (or take the underpass), and walk toward Schützenstrasse, which marks the start of Munich's pedestrian shopping mall, the Fussgängerzone, 2 km (1 mi) of traffic-free streets. Running virtually the length of Schützenstrasse is Munich's largest department store, Hertie. At the end of the street you descend via the pedestrian underpass into another shopping empire, a vast underground complex of boutiques and cafés. Above you is the busy traffic intersection, **Karlsplatz** ②, known locally as Stachus, with a popular fountain area.

Ahead stands one of the city's oldest gates, the Karlstor, first mentioned in local records in 1302. Beyond it lies Munich's main shopping thoroughfare, Neuhauserstrasse, and its extension, Kaufingerstrasse. On your left as you enter Neuhauserstrasse is another attractive Munich fountain: a jovial, late-19th-century figure of Bacchus. Neuhauserstrasse and Kaufingerstrasse are a jumble of ancient and modern buildings. This part of town was bombed almost to extinction during World War II and has been extensively rebuilt. Great efforts were made to ensure that the designs of these new buildings harmonized with the rest of the old city, although some of the newer structures are little more than functional. Still, even though this may not be an architectural high point of the city, there are at least some redeeming features. Haus Oberpollinger, on Neuhauserstrasse, is one; it's a department store hiding behind an imposing 19th-century facade. Notice the weather vanes of old merchant ships on its high-gabled roof.

Shopping, however, is not the only attraction on these streets. Worldly department stores rub shoulders with two remarkable churches: the **Bürgersaal** ③ and the **Michaelskirche** ④. The 16th-century Michaelskirche was the first Renaissance church of this size in southern Germany. Its fanciful Renaissance facade contrasts finely with the baroque exterior of the Bürgersaal.

The massive building next to Michaelskirche was once one of Munich's oldest churches, built during the late 13th century for Benedictine monks. It was secularized during the early 19th century, served as a warehouse for some years, and today houses the **Deutsches Jagd- und Fischereimuseum** ⑤.

Turn left here onto Augustinerstrasse and you will soon arrive in Frauenplatz, a quiet square with a shallow, sunken fountain. Towering over it is the **Frauenkirche** ⑥, Munich's cathedral, whose twin domes are at the same time the city's main landmark and its main symbol. From the cathedral follow any of the alleys heading east and you'll reach the very heart of Munich, **Marienplatz** ⑦, which is surrounded by stores and dining spots. Marienplatz is dominated by the 19th-century **Neues Rathaus** ⑧, while the **Altes Rathaus** ⑨, a medieval building of assured charm, sits modestly, as if forgotten, in a corner of the square. Its great hall—destroyed in 1944 but now fully restored—was the work of architect Jörg von Halspach.

Hungry? Thirsty? Help is only a few steps away. From the Altes Rathaus cross the street, passing the Heiliggeistkirche, an early Munich church with a rococo interior added between 1724 and 1730. Heiliggeiststrasse brings you to the jumble of market stalls known as the **Viktualienmarkt** ⑩, the city's open-air food market.

From the market follow Rosental into Sendlingerstrasse, one of the city's most interesting shopping streets, and head left toward Sendlinger Tor, a finely restored medieval brick gate. On your right as you head down Sendlingerstrasse is the remarkable 18th-century Church of St. Johann Nepomuk, known as the **Asamkirche** ⑪ because of the two Asam brothers, Cosmas Damian and Egid Quirin, who built it. The exterior fits so snugly into the street's housefronts (the Asam brothers lived next door) that you might easily overlook the church as you pass; yet the raw rock foundation of the facade, with its gigantic pilasters, announces the presence of something unusual.

From the Asamkirche return down Sendlingerstrasse toward the city center and turn right into the Rindermarkt (the former cattle market), and you'll be beneath the soaring tower of **Peterskirche** ⑫, or Alter Peter (Old Peter), the city's oldest and best-loved parish church. From Peterskirche reenter Marienplatz and pass in front of the Altes Rathaus once again to step into Burgstrasse. You'll soon find yourself in the quiet, airy **Alter Hof** ⑬, the inner courtyard of the original palace of the Wittelsbach rulers of Bavaria.

12

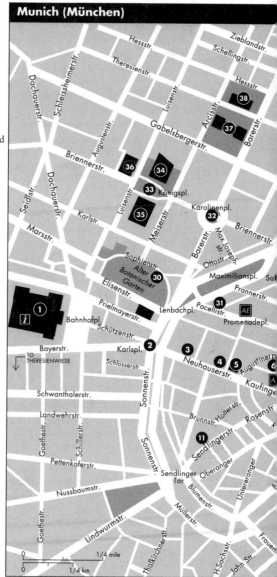

Munich (München)

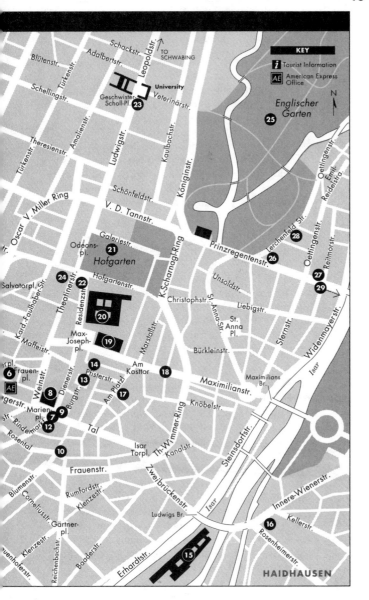

KEY

i Tourist Information

AE American Express Office

N

Englischer Garten 25

TO SCHWABING

Schackstr.

Adalbertstr.

Blütenstr.

Türkenstr.

Schellingstr.

University

Leopoldstr.

Geschwister-Scholl-Pl. 23

Veterinärstr.

Theresienstr.

Amalienstr.

Ludwigstr.

Kaulbachstr.

Königinstr.

Türkenstr.

Schönfeldstr.

V. Miller Ring

Oscar

V. D. Tannstr.

Oettingenstr.

Emil-Riedelstr.

Lerchenfeld Str.

28

Galeriestr.

Odeons-pl.

Hofgarten

21

K-Scharnagl-Ring

Prinzregentenstr.

26

Oettingenstr.

Reitmorstr.

Hofgartenstr.

Salvatorpl.

24

22

Theatinerstr.

Residenzstr.

Unsoldstr.

27

29

Kard.-Faulhaber-Str.

20

Christophstr.

St.-Anna-Str.

Liebigstr.

Sternstr.

Maffeistr.

Max-Joseph-pl.

19

Marstallstr.

St. Anna Pl.

Widenmayerstr.

Isar

14

Am Kosttor

18

Bürkleinstr.

6

Frauen-pl.

AE

8

Dienerstr.

Pfisterstr.

13

Burgstr.

17

Maximilianstr.

Maximilians Br.

gerstr.

Marien-pl.

9

7

Am Platzl

Knöbelstr.

12

Tal

Steinsdorfstr.

Rosental

Rindermarkt

10

Isar Torpl.

Th-Wimmer-Ring

Kanalstr.

Innere-Wienerstr.

Blumenstr.

Frauenstr.

Kellerstr.

Rumfordstr.

Zweibrückenstr.

Klenzestr.

16

Corneliusstr.

Gärtner-pl.

Ludwigs Br.

Isar

Rosenheimerstr.

Reichenbachstr.

Klenzestr.

Baaderstr.

15

auenhoferstr.

Erhardtstr.

HAIDHAUSEN

A short distance beyond the northern archway of the Alter Hof, on the right-hand side of Pfisterstrasse, stands the former royal mint, the **Münze** ⑭.

If you'd like to visit some museums, extend your walk by about 10 minutes, returning down Burgstrasse to broad Tal, once an important trading route that entered Munich at the Isartor, now beautifully restored to its original medieval appearance. Continue across Isartorplatz into Zweibrückenstrasse, and you'll come to the Isar River. There on a river island is the massive bulk of the **Deutsches Museum** ⑮, with a gigantic thermometer and barometer on its tower showing the way to the main entrance. Budding scientists and young dreamers alike will be delighted by its extensive collections and its many activities that provide buttons to push and cranks to turn.

On a rainy day you can pack your swimwear and splash around in the setting of the Müllersches Volksbad, a restored Jugendstil indoor swimming pool at Ludwigsbrücke, opposite the Deutsches Museum. On a sunny day join the locals for ice cream and a stroll along the Isar River, where the more daring sunbathe nude on pebble islands. Or walk up the hill from the Volksbad and see what art exhibition or avant-garde film (often in English) is showing at the modern, redbrick **Gasteig Culture Center** ⑯.

TIMING

Set aside at least a whole morning for this walk, arranging to be in Marienplatz when the Glockenspiel (chiming clock) plays at 11 or noon. The churches along the route will each demand at least a half hour of your time. You'll also be tempted to look into one or more of the department stores in the pedestrian shopping zone, so if it's noon by the time you get to Marienplatz, step into the nearby Viktualienmarkt for a stand-up lunch at any of the many stalls. Prepare for big crowds in Marienplatz when the Glockenspiel (chiming clock) plays, and try to avoid shopping between noon and 2, when German workers grab a lunch break and make for the department stores. If hunting, shooting, and fishing are your thing, you'll spend at least two hours in the Deutsches Jagd- und Fischereimuseum.

Sights to See

⑬ Alter Hof (Old Palace). This palace was the original residence of the Wittelsbach rulers of Bavaria, who held court starting in 1253. The palace now serves as local government offices. Something of the medieval flavor of those times has survived in the Alter Hof's quiet courtyard in the otherwise busy downtown area. Don't pass through without turning to admire the medieval oriel (bay window) that hides modestly on the south wall, just around the corner as you enter the courtyard.

⑨ Altes Rathaus (Old City Hall). This was Munich's first city hall, built in 1474 and restored after wartime bomb damage. Its fine assembly hall is used for official receptions. The tower provides a satisfyingly atmospheric setting for a little toy museum, accessible via a winding staircase. It includes several exhibits from the United States. ⊠ *Marienpl.* 🖂 *DM 5.* ☉ *Daily 10–5:30.*

★ ⑪ Asamkirche (Asam Church). Munich's most unusual church has a suitably extraordinary entrance, framed by raw rock foundations. The insignificant church door, crammed between its craggy shoulders, gives little idea of the splendor within. Before you enter, have a look above the doorway at the statue of St. Nepomuk, a 14th-century Bohemian monk who drowned in the Danube; you'll see that angels are conducting him to heaven from a rocky riverbank. Inside you'll discover a prime example of true southern German, late-Baroque architecture. Red stucco and rosy marble cover the walls; there is an explosion of frescoes, statuary, and gilding. The little church overwhelms with its opulence and lavish detailing—take a look at the gilt skeletons in the little atrium—and creates a powerfully mystical atmosphere. ⊠ *Sendlingerstr.* ☉ *Daily 9–5:30.*

❸ Bürgersaal (Citizens' Hall). Beneath the modest roof of this unassuming church are two contrasting levels. The Oberkiche upper level—the church proper—consists of a richly decorated Baroque oratory. Its elaborate stucco foliage and paintings of Bavarian places of pilgrimage project a distinctly different ambience from that of the Unterkirche lower level, reached by descending a double staircase. This gloomy, crypt-like chamber contains the tomb of Rupert Mayer, a famous Jesuit priest renowned for his energetic and outspoken opposition to the Nazis. ⊠ *Neuhauserstr. 14,* ☎ *089/223–884.* ☉ *Oberkirche Mon.–Sat. 11–1, Sun. 9–12:30; Unterkirche Mon.–Sat. 6:30 AM–7 PM, Sun. 7–7.*

❺ Deutsches Jagd- und Fischereimuseum (German Museum of Hunting and Fishing). Lovers of the thrill of the chase will be fascinated by this museum. It contains the world's largest collection of fishhooks, some 500 stuffed animals (including a 6½-ft-tall North American grizzly bear), a 12,000-year-old skeleton of an Irish deer, and a valuable collection of hunting weapons. ⊠ *Neuhauserstr. 2,* ☎ *089/220–522.* ▣ *DM 5.* ☉ *Tues., Wed., and Fri.–Sun. 9:30–5; Mon. and Thurs. 9:30–9.*

★ ☾ **⓯ Deutsches Museum** (German Museum of Science and Technology). Founded in 1903 and housed in its present monumental building since 1925, this is one of the most stimulating and innovative science museums in Europe. Nineteen km (12 mi) of corridors, six floors of exhibits, and 30 departments make up the immense collections. Set aside a full day if you plan to do justice to the entire museum. The technically most advanced planetarium in Europe was recently opened within this huge museum complex. The planetarium has up to six shows daily, including a Laser Magic display. The old Deutsches Museum concert hall now houses an IMAX theater—a wraparound screen six stories high showing documentary films in which spectators feel as if they're part of the action. There are up to 14 performances daily. An Internet Café has taken a home on the third floor of the Deutsches Museum and is open daily 9–3. ⊠ *Museumsinsel 1,* ☎ *089/21791, 089/211–25180 to reserve tickets at planetarium and IMAX.* ▣ *Museum DM 10, planetarium DM 11.90, IMAX DM 11.90; combined ticket DM 20.50 (admission for some performances is higher).* ☉ *Daily 9 AM–11 PM.*

....

OFF THE
BEATEN
PATH

FRANZISKANERKLOSTERKIRCHE ST. ANNA (Franciscan Monastery Church of St. Anna) – This striking example of the two Asam brothers' work may be found in the city district of Lehel. Though less opulently decorated than the Asamkirche, this small Franciscan monastery church, consecrated in 1737, impresses with its sense of movement and its heroic scale. It was largely rebuilt after wartime bomb damage.

The ceiling fresco by Cosmas Damian Asam was removed before World War II and, after restoration, now glows in all its original vivid joyfulness. The ornate altar was also designed by the Asam brothers. Towering over the delicate little church, on the opposite side of the street, is the neo-Romanesque bulk of the 19th-century church of St. Anna—the contrast between the two churches is startling. You can get to Lehel on Tram 17 or U-bahn 4 or 5 from the city center. ⊠ *St.-Anna-Str.,* ☎ *089/212–1820.*

★ ❻ **Frauenkirche** (Church of Our Lady). Munich's cathedral, or Dom, is a distinctive late-Gothic brick structure with two enormous towers, which are Munich's main landmark and city symbol. Each is more than 300 ft high, and both are capped by very un-Gothic onion-shape domes. Some observers say the towers look like overflowing beer mugs.

The main body of the cathedral was completed in 20 years (1474–94)—a record time in those days. The towers were added, almost as an afterthought, between 1524 and 1525. Jörg von Polling, the Frauenkirche's original architect, is buried within the walls of the cathedral. The building suffered severe damage during the Allied bombing of Munich and was lovingly restored from 1947 to 1957. Inside, the church combines most of von Polling's original features with a stark, clean modernity and simplicity of line, emphasized by slender, white octagonal pillars that sweep up through the nave to the yellow-traced ceiling far above. As you enter the church, look on the stone floor for the dark imprint of a large footstep—the *Teufelstritt* (Devil's footprint). According to local lore, the Devil challenged von Polling to build a nave without windows. Von Polling wagered his soul and accepted the challenge, building a cathedral that is flooded with light from 66-ft-high windows that are invisible to anyone standing at the point marked by the Teufelstritt. The cathedral houses an elaborate 15th-century black-marble memorial to Emperor Ludwig the Bavarian, guarded by four 16th-century armored knights.

A splendid view of the city is yours from an observation platform high in one of the towers. But beware—you must climb 86 steps to reach the tower elevator! ⊠ *Frauenpl.,*

☎ 089/290–0820. 🎟 *Tower DM 4.* ☉ *Tower elevator Apr.– Oct., Mon.–Sat. 10–5.*

⑯ Gasteig Culture Center. This striking postmodern brick cultural complex for music, theater, and film has an open-plan interior and a maze of interior courtyards and plazas, sitting high above the Isar River. The center has two theaters, where plays in English are occasionally performed. ⊠ *Rosenheimerstr. 5,* ☎ *089/5481–8181.*

❶ Hauptbahnhof (Main Train Station). Tourists often start their exploration here because it contains the city tourist office, with maps and helpful information on events around town. ⊠ *Bayerstr.*

❷ Karlsplatz. Known locally as Stachus, this busy intersection has one of Munich's most popular fountains, a circle of water jets that acts as a magnet on hot summer days for city shoppers and office workers seeking a cool corner. The semicircle of yellow-front buildings that back the fountain, with their high windows and delicate cast-iron balconies, gives the area a southern, almost Mediterranean, air. ⊠ *Sonnenstr., Bayerstr., Schützenstr., Luisenstr., Prielmayerstr., and Neuhauserstr.; bordered on north by Lenbachpl.*

★ ❼ Marienplatz. Surrounded by shops, restaurants, and cafés, this square is named after the gilded statue of the Virgin Mary that has been watching over it for more than three centuries. It was erected in 1638 at the behest of Elector Maximilian I as an act of thanksgiving for the survival of the city during the Thirty Years' War, the cataclysmic religious struggle that devastated vast regions of Germany. When the statue, which stands on a marble column, was taken down to be cleaned for a eucharistic world congress in 1960, workmen found a small casket in the base containing a splinter of wood said to be from the cross of Christ. ⊠ *Bounded by Kaufingerstr., Rosenstr., Weinstr., and Dienerstr.*

❹ Michaelskirche (St. Michael's Church). A curious story explains why this sturdy Renaissance church has no tower. Seven years after the start of construction the principal tower collapsed. Its patron, pious Duke Wilhelm V, regarded the disaster as a heavenly sign that the church wasn't big enough, so he ordered a change in the plans—this time without a tower. Completed seven years later, the Michaels-

kirche was the first Renaissance church of this size in southern Germany. The duke is buried in the crypt, along with
40 members of Bavaria's famous Wittelsbach family (the
ruling dynasty for seven centuries), including the eccentric
king Ludwig II. A severe neoclassical monument in the
north transept contains the tomb of Napoléon's stepson,
Eugene de Beauharnais, who married one of the daughters
of Bavaria's King Maximilian I and died in Munich in
1824. You'll find the plain white stucco interior of the
church and its slightly barnlike atmosphere soothingly simple after the lavish decoration of the nearby Bürgarsaal. ⊠
Neuhauserstr. 6, ☎ *089/551–99257.* ☉ *Mon.–Wed., Fri.,
and Sat. 8:30–7; Thurs. 8:30–9; Sun. 6 AM–10 PM; guided
tour of church Wed. at 2.*

⓮ **Münze** (Mint). Originally the royal stables, the Münze was
created by court architect Wilhelm Egkl between 1563 and
1567 and now serves as an office building. A stern neoclassical facade emblazoned with gold was added in 1809;
the interior courtyard has Renaissance-style arches. ⊠ *Pfisterstr. 4.* 🎟 *Free.* ☉ *Mon.–Thurs. 8–4, Fri. 8–2.*

➑ **Neues Rathaus** (New City Hall). Munich's present city
hall was built between 1867 and 1908 in the fussy, turreted,
neo-Gothic style so beloved by King Ludwig II. Architectural historians are divided over its merits, though its dramatic scale and lavish detailing are impressive. Perhaps
the most serious criticism is that the Dutch and Flemish style
of the building seems out of place amid the baroque and
rococo of so much of the rest of the city. In 1904 a glockenspiel (a chiming clock with mechanical figures) was
added to the tower; it plays daily at 11 AM and noon, with
additional performances at 5 PM and 9 PM June–October.
As chimes peal out over the square, doors flip open and
brightly colored dancers and jousting knights go through
their paces. They act out two events from Munich's past:
a tournament held in Marienplatz in 1568 and the *Schäf-
flertanz* (Dance of the Coopers), which commemorated
the end of the plague of 1517. When Munich was in ruins
after the war, an American soldier contributed some paint
to restore the battered figures, and he was rewarded with
a ride on one of the jousters' horses, high above the cheer-
ing crowds. You, too, can travel up there, by elevator, to

an observation point near the top of one of the towers. On a clear day the view is spectacular. ⊠ *Marienpl.,* ☎ *089/ 2331.* 🔲 *Tower DM 3.* ☉ *Mon.–Thurs. 9–4, Fri. 9–1.*

⑫ Peterskirche (St. Peter's Church). Munich's oldest and smallest parish church traces its origins to the 11th century and over the years has been restored in a variety of architectural styles. Today you'll find a rich baroque interior, with a magnificent late-Gothic high altar and aisle pillars decorated with exquisite 18th-century figures of the apostles. From the top of its 300-ft tower there's a fine view of the city. In clear weather it's well worth the climb—the view includes glimpses of the Alps to the south. Peterskirche has a Scottish priest who is glad to show English-speaking visitors around the church. ⊠ *Rindermarkt,* ☎ *089/260–4070.* 🔲 *Tower DM 2.50.* ☉ *Weekdays 9–6, Sat. 8:30–6, Sun. 10–6.*

OFF THE
BEATEN
PATH

STREETCAR 19 – For the cheapest sight-seeing tour on wheels of the city center, board this streetcar outside the ☞ **Hauptbahnhof** on Bahnhofplatz and make the 15-minute journey to Max Weber Platz. Explore the streets around the square, part of the old bohemian residential area of Haidhausen (with some of the city's best bars and restaurants), and then return by a different route on Streetcar 18 to Karlsplatz.

THERESIENWIESE – The site of Munich's annual beer festival—the infamous Oktoberfest—is only a 10-minute walk from the ☞ **Hauptbahnhof;** or by subway it is one stop on the U-4 or U-5. The Theresienwiese is an enormous exhibition ground, named after a young woman whose engagement party gave rise to the Oktoberfest. In 1810 the party celebrated the betrothal of Princess Therese von Sachsen-Hildburghausen to the Bavarian crown prince Ludwig, later Ludwig I. It was such a success, attended by nearly the entire population of Munich, that it became an annual affair. Beer was served then as now, but what began as a night out for the locals has become a 16-day international bonanza at the end of September and the beginning of October, attracting more than 6 million people each year (it qualifies as the *Oktoberfest* by ending the first Sunday in October).

Overlooking the Theresienwiese is a 19th-century hall of fame—one of the last works of Ludwig I—and a monumental bronze statue of the maiden **Bavaria,** more than 100 ft high.

The statue is hollow, and 130 steps take you up into the braided head for a view of Munich through Bavaria's eyes. 🕮 DM 3. ☉ Tues.–Sun. 10–noon and 2–4.

★ ❿ **Viktualienmarkt.** The city's open-air food market (*Viktualien* means vittles) has a wide range of produce, German and international food, Bavarian beer, and French wines, which make the area a feast for the eyes as well as the stomach. It is also the realm of the garrulous, sturdy market women, dressed in traditional country costumes, who run the stalls with dictatorial authority; one was roundly reprimanded by Munich's leading newspaper for rudely warning an American tourist not to touch the fruit!

Royal Munich

From the relatively modest palace of the Alter Hof (☞ *above*), Munich's royal rulers expanded their quarters northward, where more space was to be found than in the jumble of narrow streets of the old quarter. The Wittelsbachs built a palace more suitable for their regal pretensions and laid out a fine garden, which was off limits at first to all but the nobility. Three avenues of regal dimension radiated outward from this new center of royal rule, and fine homes arose along them. One of them—Prinzregentenstrasse—marks the southern end of Munich's huge public park, the Englischer Garten, which was also the creation of a Wittelsbach ruler.

A Good Walk

A good way to start this virtually endless walk is to stoke up first with a Bavarian breakfast of white sausage, pretzels, and beer at the suitably named **Hofbräuhaus** ⑰, perhaps Munich's best-known beer hall, on Am Platzl. Turn right from the Hofbräuhaus for the short walk along Orlandostrasse to **Maximilianstrasse** ⑱, Munich's most elegant shopping street, named after King Maximilian II, whose statue you'll see far down on the right. This wide boulevard has many grand buildings, which contain government offices and the city's ethnological museum, the **Staatliches Museum für Völkerkunde.** The Maximilianeum, on a rise beyond the Isar River, is an impressive mid-19th-century palace where the Bavarian state government now meets.

Across Maximilianstrasse as you enter from the Hofbräuhaus stands a handsome city landmark: the Hotel Vier
Jahreszeiten, a historic watering hole for princes, millionaires, and the expense-account jet set.

Turn left down Maximilianstrasse, away from the Maximilianeum, and you'll enter the square called Max-Joseph-
Platz, dominated by the pillared portico of the 19th-century
Nationaltheater ⑲, home of the Bavarian State Opera Company. The statue in the square's center is of Bavaria's first
king, Max Joseph. Along the north side of this untidily arranged square (marred by the entrance to an underground
parking lot) is the lofty and austere south wall of the **Residenz** ⑳, the royal palace of Wittelsbach rulers for more than
six centuries.

Directly north of the Residenz, on Hofgartenstrasse, lies the
former royal garden, the **Hofgarten** ㉑. You can be for-
given for any confusion about your whereabouts ("Can this
really be Germany?") when you step from the Hofgarten
onto Odeonsplatz.To your left is the 19th-century **Feldherrnhalle** ㉒, a local hall of fame modeled after a Florentine loggia.

Looking north up Ludwigstrasse, the arrow-straight avenue
that ends at the Feldherrnhalle, you'll see the **Siegestor** ㉓,
or victory arch, which marks the beginning of Leopoldstrasse. Completing this impressively Italianate panorama
is the great yellow bulk of the former royal church of St.
Kajetan, the **Theatinerkirche** ㉔, an imposing Baroque building. Its lofty towers frame a restrained facade capped by a
massive dome.

Now head north up Ludwigstrasse. The first stretch of the
street was designed by court architect Leo von Klenze. In
much the same way that Baron Haussmann would later de-
molish many of the old streets and buildings in Paris, re-
placing them with stately boulevards, so von Klenze swept
aside the small dwellings and alleys that stood here to build
his great avenue. His high-windowed and formal buildings
have never quite been accepted by Müncheners, and indeed
there's still a sense that Ludwigstrasse is an intruder. Most
visitors either love it or hate it. Von Klenze's buildings end
just before Ludwigstrasse becomes Leopoldstrasse, and it

In case you want to see the world.

At American Express, we're here to make your journey a smooth one. So we have over 1,700 travel service locations in over 120 countries ready to help. What else would you expect from the world's largest travel agency?

do more ®

AMERICAN
EXPRESS

Travel

http://www.americanexpress.com/travel

In case you want to be welcomed there.

We're here to see that you're always welcomed at establishments everywhere. That's why millions of people carry the American Express® Card – for peace of mind, confidence, and security, around the world or just around the corner.

do more ®

In case you're running low.

We're here to help with more than 118,000 Express Cash locations around the world. In order to enroll, just call American Express before you start your vacation.

do more

And just in case.

We're here with American Express® Travelers Cheques and Cheques *for Two*.® They're the safest way to carry money on your vacation and the surest way to get a refund, practically anywhere, anytime.

Another way we help you...

do more

AMERICAN EXPRESS

Travelers Cheques

is easy to see where he handed construction over to another leading architect, Friedrich von Gärtner. The severe neo-classical buildings that line southern Ludwigstrasse—including the Bayerische Staatsbibliothek (Bavarian State Library), the Universität (University), and the peculiarly Byzantine Ludwigskirche—fragment into the lighter styles of Leopoldstrasse. The more delicate structures are echoed by the busy street life you'll find here in summer. Once the hub of the legendary artists' district of Schwabing, Leopold-strasse still throbs with life from spring to fall, exuding the atmosphere of a Mediterranean boulevard, with cafés, wine terraces, and artists' stalls. In comparison, Ludwigstrasse is inhabited by ghosts of the past.

At the south end of Leopoldstrasse, beyond the Siegestor, lies the great open quadrangle of the university, Geschwis-ter-Scholl-Platz, named after brother and sister Hans and Sophie Scholl, who were executed in 1943 for leading the short-lived anti-Nazi resistance movement known as the Weisse Rose (White Rose). At its north end Leopoldstrasse leads into Schwabing itself, once Munich's Bohemian quarter but now distinctly upscale. Explore the streets of old Schwabing around Wedekindplatz to get the feel of the place. (Those in search of the Bohemian mood that once animated Schwabing should head to Haidhausen, on the other side of the Isar.)

Bordering the east side of Schwabing is the **Englischer Garten** ㉕. Five km (3 mi) long and 1½ km (about 1 mi) wide, it's Germany's largest city park, stretching from the Prinzre-gentenstrasse, the broad avenue laid out by Prince Regent Luitpold at the end of the 19th century, to the city's northern boundary, where the lush parkland is taken over by the rough embrace of open countryside. Dominating the park's southern border is one of the few examples of Hitler-era architecture still standing in Munich: the colonnaded Haus der Kunst (House of Art), home of the **Staatsgalerie Moderner Kunst**—and also of Munich's most fashionable disco, the PI.

A few hundred yards farther along Prinzregentenstrasse are two other leading museums, the **Bayerisches Nationalmu-seum** ㉖ and the **Schack-Galerie** ㉗, while around the first left-hand corner, on Lerchenfeldstrasse, is a museum of prehistory that brings the ancient past to life in fascinating form, the **Prähistorische Staatssammlung** ㉘.

The column you see standing triumphant on a hill at the eastern end of Prinzregentenstrasse, just across the Isar River from the Schack-Galerie, is Munich's well-loved Friedensengel (Angel of Peace). This striking gilded angel crowns a marble column in a small park overlooking the Isar River and marks one end of Prinzregentenstrasse. Just across the river, beyond the Friedensengel, is another historic home, which became a major Munich art gallery— the **Museum Villa Stuck** ㉙, a jewel of art nouveau fantasy.

There are innumerable walks here along the banks of the Isar River and in the nearby Englischer Garten, where you have the choice of ending your stroll with a stop at one of its three beer gardens (the Chinese Tower is the largest and most popular) or with a visit to the Seehaus, on the banks of the park's lake, the Kleinhesseloher See. Here you'll have another choice to make: a smart restaurant or a cozy *Bierstube* (pub).

TIMING

You'll need a day (and good walking shoes) for this stroll, which ends in the virtually endless Englischer Garten. Set aside at least two hours for a tour of the Residenz. If the weather is fine, try to return to the southern end of the Englischer Garten at dusk, when you'll be treated to an unforgettable silhouette of the Munich skyline, black against the retreating light.

Sights to See

㉖ **Bayerisches Nationalmuseum** (Bavarian National Museum). The extensive collection here contains Bavarian and other German art and artifacts. The highlight for some will be the medieval and Renaissance wood carvings, with many works by the great Renaissance sculptor Tilman Riemenschneider. Fine tapestries, arms and armor, a unique collection of Christmas crèches (the Krippenschau), Bavarian arts and crafts, and folk artifacts compete for your attention. Although the Bayerisches Nationalmuseum places emphasis on Bavarian cultural history, it has exhibits of outstanding international importance and stages regular exhibitions that attract worldwide attention. ✉ *Prinzre-*

gentenstr. 3, ☎ *089/211–241.* ☞ *DM 3, DM 8 for special exhibitions.* ☉ *Tues.–Sun. 9:30–5.*

★ ㉕ **Englischer Garten** (English Garden). This virtually endless park, which is embraced by open countryside at Munich's northern city limits, was designed for the Bavarian prince Karl Theodor by a refugee from the American War of Independence, Count Rumford. Although Rumford was of English descent, it was the open, informal nature of the park—reminiscent of the rolling parklands with which English aristocrats of the 18th century liked to surround their country homes—that determined its name. It has an appealing boating lake, four beer gardens, and a series of curious decorative and monumental constructions, including the Monopteros, a Greek temple designed by von Klenze for King Ludwig I and built on an artificial hill in the southern section of the park. In the center of one of the park's most popular beer gardens is a Chinese pagoda erected in 1789, destroyed during the war, and then reconstructed. The Chinese Tower beer garden is world famous, but the park has prettier places for downing a beer: the Aumeister, for example, along the northern perimeter. The Aumeister's restaurant is in an early 19th-century hunting lodge.

The Englischer Garten is a paradise for joggers, cyclists, and, in winter, cross-country skiers. The Munich Cricket Club grounds are in the southern section—proof, perhaps, that even that most British of games is not invulnerable to the single-minded Germans—and spectators are welcome. The park also has specially designated areas for nude sunbathing—the Germans have a positively pagan attitude toward the sun—so don't be surprised to see naked bodies bordering the flower beds and paths.

㉒ **Feldherrnhalle** (Generals' Hall). This local hall of fame was modeled on the 14th-century Loggia dei Lanzi in Florence. In the '30s and '40s it was a key Nazi shrine, marking the site of Hitler's abortive rising, or putsch, which took place in 1923. All who passed it had to give the Nazi salute. ✉ *South end of Odeonspl.*

⑰ **Hofbräuhaus.** Duke Wilhelm V founded Munich's most famous brewery in 1589, and although it still boasts royal patronage in its title, it's now state-owned. If the downstairs hall is too noisy for you, try the quiet restaurant upstairs. Beer is what you're expected to order here. Hofbräu means "royal brew," a term that aptly describes the golden beer served here in king-size liter mugs. ⊠ *Am Platzl 9,* ☎ *089/221–676.*

㉑ Hofgarten (Royal Garden). Two sides of the pretty, formal garden that was once part of the royal palace grounds are bordered by arcades designed during the 19th century by the royal architect Leo von Klenze. On the east side of the garden stands the new state chancellery, built around the ruins of the 19th-century Army Museum and incorporating the remains of a Renaissance arcade. Its most prominent feature is a large copper dome. Bombed during World War II air raids, the museum stood untouched for almost 40 years as a grim reminder of the war.

In front of the chancellery stands one of Europe's most unusual—some say most effective—war memorials. Instead of looking up at the monument, you are led down to it—it is a sunken crypt covered by a massive granite block. In the crypt lies a German soldier from World War I. ⊠ *Hofgartenstr., north of Residenz.*

The monument is a stark contrast to another, more recent memorial that stands unobtrusively in front of the northern wing of the chancellery: a simple cube of black marble bearing inscriptions of hand-written wartime manifestos by leading anti-Nazis, including members of the White Rose movement.

Ludwigskirche (Ludwig's Church). Planted halfway along the severe, neoclassical Ludwigstrasse is this curious neo-Byzantine/early Renaissance–style church. It was built at the behest of Ludwig I to provide his newly completed suburb with a parish church. Though most visitors will find the building a curiosity at best, it can be worth a stop to see the fresco of the *Last Judgment* in the choir. At 60 ft by 37 ft, it is one of the world's largest. ⊠ *Ludwigstr. 22,* ☎ *089/288–334.* ⊙ *Daily 7–7.*

⑱ Maximilianstrasse. Munich's sophisticated shopping street was named after King Maximilian II, who wanted to break away from the Greek-influenced classical style of city architecture favored by his father, Ludwig I, so he ingenuously asked his cabinet whether he could be allowed to create something original. Maximilianstrasse was the result. This broad boulevard, its central stretch lined with majestic buildings (now government offices and the city's ethnological museum, the ☞ **Staatliches Museum für Völkerkunde**), culminates on a rise beyond the Isar River in the stately outlines of the **Maximilianeum,** a lavish 19th-century arcaded palace built for Maximilian II as part of an ambitious city-planning scheme and now the home of the Bavarian state parliament. Today only the terrace can be visited.

㉙ **Museum Villa Stuck.** This museum is the former home of one of Munich's leading turn-of-the-century artists, Franz von Stuck. His work covers the walls of the haunting rooms of the neoclassical villa, which is also used for regular art exhibits organized by the museum's Australian director. ✉ *Prinzregentenstr. 60,* ☎ *089/455–5510.* ≦ *DM 6 and up, according to exhibit.* ☉ *Tues., Wed., and Fri.–Sun. 10–5; Thurs. 10–9.*

⑲ **Nationaltheater** (National Theater). Built in the late 19th century as a royal opera house in the classical style, with a pillared portico, this large theater was bombed during the war but is now restored to its original splendor. It has some of the world's most advanced stage technology.

㉘ **Prähistorische Staatssammlung** (State Prehistoric Collection). This is Bavaria's principal record of its prehistoric, Roman, and Celtic past. The perfectly preserved body of a young girl who was ritually sacrificed, recovered from a Bavarian peat moor, is among its more spine-chilling exhibits. Head down to the basement to see the fine Roman mosaic floor. ✉ *Lerchenfeldstr. 2,* ☎ *089/293–911.* ≦ *DM 5.* ☉ *Tues., Wed., and Fri.–Sun. 9–4; Thurs. 9–8.*

★ ⑳ **Residenz** (Royal Palace). Munich's royal palace began as a small castle, to which the Wittelsbach dukes moved in the 14th century, when the Alter Hof became surrounded by the teeming tenements of an expanding Munich. In succeeding centuries the royal residence developed parallel to the importance, requirements, and interests of its occupants. As the complex expanded, it came to include the Königsbau (on Max-Josef-Platz) and then (clockwise) the

Alte Residenz; the Festsaal (Banquet Hall); the Altes Residenztheater (Cuvilliés Theater); Allerheiligenhofkirche (All Soul's Church, now ruined); the Residenz theater; and the Nationaltheater.

Building began in 1385 with the **Neuveste** (New Fortress), which comprised the northeast section; most of it burned to the ground in 1750, but one of its finest rooms survived: the 16th-century **Antiquarium,** which was built for Duke Albrecht V's collection of antique statues (today it's used chiefly for state receptions). The throne room of King Ludwig I, the **Neuer Herkulessaal,** is now a concert hall. The accumulated treasures of the Wittelsbachs can be seen in the **Schatzkammer,** or treasury (one rich centerpiece is a small Renaissance statue of St. George, studded with 2,291 diamonds, 209 pearls, and 406 rubies), and a representative collection of paintings and tapestries is housed in the **Residenzmuseum.** Antique coins and Egyptian works of art are in the two other museums of this vast palace. In the center of the complex, entered through an inner courtyard where chamber-music concerts are given in summer, is a small rococo theater, built by François Cuvilliés from 1751 to 1755. The French-born Cuvilliés was a dwarf who was admitted to the Bavarian court as a decorative "bauble." Prince Max Emanuel recognized his latent artistic ability and had him trained as an architect. The prince's eye for talent gave Germany some of its richest rococo treasures. ✉ *Max-Joseph-Pl. 3,* ☎ *089/290–671. Treasury and Residenzmuseum,* 🎟 *DM 5.* ☉ *Tues.–Sun. 10–4:30. Staatliche Münzsammlung (coin collection),* ✉ *entrance at Residenzstr. 1,* 🎟 *DM 4, free Sun.* ☉ *Tues.–Sun. 10–4:30. Staatliche Sammlung Ägyptischer Kunst (Egyptian art),* ✉ *Hofgarten entrance to Residenz,* 🎟 *DM 5, free Sun.* ☉ *Tues. 9–9, Wed.–Fri. 9–4, weekends 10–5. Cuvilliés Theater,* 🎟 *DM 3.* ☉ *Mon.–Sat. 2–5, Sun. 10–5.*

㉗ Schack-Galerie. Those with a taste for florid and romantic 19th-century German paintings will appreciate the collections of the Schack-Galerie, originally the private collection of one Count Schack. Others may find the gallery dull, filled with plodding and repetitive works by painters who now repose in well-deserved obscurity. ✉ *Prinzregentenstr. 9,* ☎ *089/238–05224.* 🎟 *DM 4 .* ☉ *Wed.–Mon. 10–5.*

㉓ **Siegestor** (Victory Arch). Marking the beginning of Leopold-strasse, the Siegestor has Italian origins—it was modeled on the Arch of Constantine in Rome—and was built to honor the achievements of the Bavarian army during the Wars of Liberation (1813–15).

Staatliches Museum für Völkerkunde (State Museum of Ethnology). Arts and crafts from around the world are displayed in this extensive museum. There are also regular ethnological exhibits. ⊠ *Maximilianstr. 42,* ☎ *089/210–1360.* 🎫 *DM 5.* ☉ *Tues.–Sun. 9:30–4:30.*

Staatsgalerie Moderner Kunst (State Gallery of Modern Art). The gallery is in the west wing of the Hitler-era Haus der Kunst (1938), a monumental pillared building at the south end of the Englischer Garten (☞ *above*) (the east wing has regularly changing exhibits). It features one of the finest collections of 20th-century paintings and sculptures in the world, including works by artists of the Blauer Reiter movement (Kandinsky, Klee, and Macke) and the Brücke movement (Heckel, Kirchner, and Nolde). ⊠ *Prinzregentenstr. 1,* ☎ *089/211–270.* 🎫 *DM 6.* ☉ *Tues., Wed., and Fri.–Sun. 10–5; Thurs. 10–8.*

㉔ **Theatinerkirche** (Theatiner Church). This mighty Baroque church owes its Italian appearance to its founder, Princess Henriette Adelaide, who commissioned it as an act of thanksgiving for the birth of her son and heir, Max Emanuel, in 1663. A native of Turin, the princess distrusted Bavarian architects and builders and thus summoned a master builder from Bologna, Agostino Barelli, to construct her church. He took as his model the Roman mother church of the newly formed Theatine Order. Barelli worked on the building for 11 years but was dismissed before the project was completed. It was another 100 years before the Theatinerkirche was finished. Step inside to admire its austere stucco interior. ⊠ *Theatinerstr. 22,* ☎ *089/221–650.* ☉ *Daily 7–7.*

NEED A BREAK?   Munich's oldest café, the renamed **Tambosi** (⊠ Odeonspl., ☎ 089/298–322), is across from the Theatinerkirche on the busy square, Odeonsplatz. In summer you have the choice of watching the hustle and bustle from a pavement table or retreating through a gate in the Hofgarten's western wall to the café's quiet, tree-shaded beer garden.

The Maxvorstadt and Schwabing

Here is the artistic center of Munich: Schwabing, the old artists' quarter, and the neighboring Maxvorstadt, where most of the city's leading art galleries and museums are congregated. Schwabing is no longer the Bohemian area where such diverse residents as Lenin and Kandinsky were once neighbors, but at least the solid cultural foundations of the Maxvorstadt are immutable. Where the two areas meet (in the streets behind the university) life hums with a creative vibrancy that is difficult to detect elsewhere in Munich.

A Good Walk

Begin with a stroll through the city's old botanical garden, the **Alter Botanischer Garten** ㉚. The grand-looking building opposite the entrance to the botanical garden is the Palace of Justice, law courts built in 1897 in suitable awe-inspiring dimensions. Across the square, at one corner of busy Lenbachplatz, you can't fail to notice one of Munich's most impressive fountains: the monumental late-19th-century Wittelsbacher Brunnen. Beyond the fountain, across neighboring Lenbachplatz in Pacellistrasse, is the Baroque **Dreifaltigkeitskirche** ㉛.

Leave the Alter Botanischer Garten at its northern end and walk up Meiserstrasse, passing on the right-hand side two solemn neoclassical buildings, one of which houses a fascinating collection of drawings and prints from the late-Gothic period to the present day. The neighboring building is the Music Academy, site of the signing of the pre-war pact carving up Czechoslovakia, by Hitler, Mussolini, Britain's Chamberlain, and France's Deladier.

At the junction of Meiserstrasse and Briennerstrasse look right to see Munich's Egyptian obelisk dominating the circular **Karolinenplatz** ㉜. On your left, at the crossroads of Meiserstrasse and Briennerstrasse, is an expansive square, **Königsplatz** ㉝, lined on three sides with the monumental Grecian-style buildings that house two museums, the **Glyptothek** ㉞ and the **Antikensammlungen** ㉟.

Turn right into Luisenstrasse after leaving Königsplatz, and you'll arrive at one of Munich's most delightful art galleries, the **Städtische Galerie im Lenbachhaus** ㊱, a Florentine-style villa containing an outstanding collection of works from the Gothic period to the present. Continue down Luisenstrasse, turning right on Theresienstrasse to reach Munich's two leading art galleries, the **Alte Pinakothek** ㊲ and the **Neue Pinakothek** ㊳, opposite it. They are as complementary as their buildings are contrasting: the Alte Pinakothek severe and serious in style, the Neue Pinakothek almost frivolously Florentine.

After a few hours immersed in culture, end your walk with a leisurely stroll through the neighboring streets of Schwabing, lined with boutiques, bars, and restaurants. If it's a fine day, head for the **Elisabethmarkt,** Schwabing's permanent market.

TIMING

This walk may take an entire day, depending on how long you're tempted to linger at the several major museums en route. Avoid the museum crowds by timing your visits as early in the day as possible. All Munich seems to discover an interest in art on Sunday, particularly during foul weather, so take a day off then from culture and join the late-breakfast and brunch crowd at the Elisabethmarkt or a brewery beer garden in good weather and at any of the many bars and Gaststätten if the weather does turn bad. Some of them have Sunday-morning jazz concerts. Many Schwabing bars have happy hours between 6 and 8—a tip for those who want to time the end of their walk with a watering-hole stop.

Sights to See

㊲ **Alte Pinakothek** (Old Picture Gallery). The towering brick Alte Pinakothek was constructed by von Klenze between 1826 and 1836 to exhibit the collection of Old Masters begun by Duke Wilhelm IV during the 16th century. It's now judged one of the world's great picture galleries. The gallery's most famous works include Dürers, Rembrandts, Rubenses, and two celebrated Murillos. The huge building was completely renovated between 1993 and 1997 and is now able to show all its treasures in suitable style. ⊠ *Barerstr. 27,* ☎ *089/238–050.* ⊠ *DM 7.* ☉ *Tues. and Thurs. 10–8, Wed. and Fri.–Sun. 10–5.*

30 **Alter Botanischer Garten** (Old Botanical Garden). Munich's first botanical garden began as the site of a huge glass palace, built here in 1853 for Germany's first industrial exhibition. In 1931 the immense structure burned down; six years later the garden was redesigned as a public park. Two features from the '30s remain: a small, square **exhibition hall,** still used for art shows; and the 1933 **Neptune Fountain,** an enormous work in the heavy, monumental style of the prewar years. At the international electricity exhibition of 1882, the world's first high-tension electricity cable was run from the park to a Bavarian village 48 km (30 mi) away. ⊠ *Entrance at Lenbachpl.*

NEED A BREAK? Tucked away on the north edge of the Alter Botanischer Garten is one of the city's central beer gardens. It's part of the **Park Café** (⊠ Sophienstr. 7, ☎ 089/598–313), which at night becomes a fashionable disco serving magnums of champagne for DM 1,500 apiece. Prices in the beer garden are more realistic.

35 **Antikensammlungen** (Antiquities Collection). This museum at Köningsplatz has a fine group of smaller sculptures, Etruscan art, Greek vases, gold, and glass. ⊠ *Königspl. 1,* ☎ *089/598–359.* 🎫 *DM 6; combined ticket to Antikensammlungen and Glyptothek DM 10.* ⊘ *Tues. and Thurs.– Sun. 10–5, Wed. 10–8; tour every other Wed. at 6.*

31 **Dreifaltigkeitskirche** (Church of the Holy Trinity). This striking Baroque edifice was built between 1711 and 1718 after a local woman prophesied doom for the city unless a new church was erected. It has heroic frescoes by Cosmas Damian Asam. ⊠ *Pacellistr. 10,* ☎ *089/290–0820.* 🎫 *Daily tour DM 5.* ⊘ *Daily 7–7.*

Elisabethmarkt (Elisabeth Market). Schwabing's permanent market is smaller than the popular Viktualienmarkt but hardly less colorful. It has a pocket-size beer garden, where a jazz band performs every Saturday from spring to autumn. ⊠ *Arcistr. and Elisabethstr.*

34 **Glyptothek.** This museum at Königsplatz features a permanent exhibition of Greek and Roman sculptures. ⊠ *Königspl. 3,* ☎ *089/286–100.* 🎫 *DM 6; combined ticket to Glyptothek and Antikensammlungen DM 10.* ⊘ *Tues.,*

Wed., and Fri.–Sun. 10–5; Thurs. 10–8; tour every other Thurs. at 6.

㉜ Karolinenplatz (Caroline Square). At the junction of Meiserstrasse and Briennerstrasse, this circular area is dominated by an Egyptian obelisk, which was unveiled in 1812 as a memorial to Bavarians killed fighting Napoléon. **Amerikahaus** (America House) faces Karolinenplatz. It has an extensive library and a year-round program of cultural events. ⊠ *Karolinenpl. 3,* ☎ *089/552–5370.*

㉝ Königsplatz (King's Square). This expansive square is lined on three sides with the monumental Grecian-style buildings by Leo von Klenze that gave Munich the nickname "Athens on the Isar." The two templelike buildings he had constructed there are now the ☞ **Glyptothek** and the ☞ **Antikensammlungen** museums. In the '30s the great parklike square was laid with granite slabs, which resounded with the thud of jackboots as the Nazis commandeered the area for their rallies. Only recently were the slabs removed; since then the square has taken on something of the green and peaceful appearance originally intended by Ludwig I.

㉟ Neue Pinakothek (New Picture Gallery). This exhibition space was opened in 1981 to house the royal collection of modern art left homeless when its former building was destroyed in the war. It's a low brick building that combines high-tech and Italianate influences in equal measure. From outside, the museum does not seem to measure up to the standards set by so many of Munich's other great public buildings. Yet the interior offers a magnificent environment for picture gazing, at least partly due to the superb natural light flooding in from the skylights. The highlights of the collection are probably the Impressionist and other French 19th-century works—Monet, Degas, and Manet are all well represented. But there's also a substantial collection of 19th-century German and Scandinavian paintings—misty landscapes predominate—that are only now coming to be recognized as admirable and worthy products of their time. ⊠ *Barerstr. 29,* ☎ *089/238–05195.* 🎟 *DM 7.* ☉ *Tues. and Thurs. 10–8, Wed. and Fri.–Sun. 10–5.*

㊱ Städtische Galerie im Lenbachhaus (Municipal Gallery). You'll find an internationally renowned picture collection inside a delightful late-19th-century Florentine-style villa, former home and studio of the artist Franz von Lenbach. It contains a rich collection of works from the Gothic period to the present, including an exciting assemblage of art from the early 20th-century *Blaue Reiter* (Blue Rider) group: Kandinsky, Klee, Jawlensky, Macke, Marc, and Münter. ⊠ *Luisenstr. 33,* ☎ *089/233–32002.* ⊡ *DM 8.* ⊙ *Tues.–Sun. 10–6.*

Outside the Center

BMW Museum. On the eastern edge of the Olympiapark (☞ *below*), you can't miss this museum, a circular tower building that looks as if it served as a set for *Star Wars.* Munich is the home of the famous car firm, and the museum contains a dazzling collection of BMWs old and new; it adjoins the BMW factory. ⊠ *Petuelring 130, U-bahn 3 to Petuelring,* ☎ *089/382–23307.* ⊡ *DM 5.50.* ⊙ *Daily 9–5, last entry at 4.*

Botanischer Garten (Botanical Garden). A collection of 14,000 plants, including orchids, cacti, cyads, Alpine flowers, and rhododendrons, makes up one of the most extensive botanical gardens in Europe. The garden lies on the eastern edge of ☞ **Schloss Nymphenburg** park. Take Tram 12 or Bus 41 from the city center to the garden. ⊠ *Menzingerstr. 65,* ☎ *089/1786–1350.* ⊡ *DM 4.* ⊙ *Oct.–Mar., daily 9–4:30; Apr.–Sept. daily 9–7:30; hothouses daily 9–noon and 1–4.*

☾ **Geiselgasteig Movie Studios.** Munich is Germany's leading moviemaking center, and from March through October the studios at Geiselgasteig, on the southern outskirts of the city, open their doors to visitors. A "Filmexpress" transports you on a 1½-hour tour of the sets of *Das Boot* (*The Boat*), *Die Unendliche Geschichte* (*The Neverending Story*), and other productions. Children should enjoy the stunt shows (mid-Apr.–Oct., weekends at 11:30, 1, and 2:30) or the newly opened "Showscan" super-wide-screen cinema. Take the U-bahn 1 or 2 from the city center to Silberhornstrasse and then change to Tram 25 to Bavariafilmplatz. ☎ *089/649–3767.* ⊡ *DM 14; stunt show DM 9;*

combined ticket for studio tour, stunt show, and Showscan cinema DM 28. ☉ *Mar.–Oct., daily 9–5; last tour at 4.*

☾ **Hellabrun Zoo.** On the southern edge of the city, this is one of the most attractive zoos in Germany. There's a minimum of cages and many parklike enclosures. Animals are arranged according to their geographical origin. The zoo's 170 acres include restaurants and children's areas. Take Bus 52 from Marienplatz or the U-bahn 3 to Thalkirchen. ✉ *Tierparkstr. 30,* ☎ *089/625–080.* 🎟 *DM 10.* ☉ *Apr.–Sept., daily 8–6; Oct.–Mar., daily 9–5.*

Olympiapark (Olympic Park). The undulating circus tent–like roofs that cover the stadia built for the 1972 Olympic Games are unobtrusively tucked away in what is now known as Olympiapark on the northern edge of Schwabing. The roofs are made of translucent tiles that glisten in the midday sun and act as amplifiers for such visiting rock bands as the Rolling Stones. Tours of the park on a Disneyland-style train run throughout the day from April through November. Take the elevator up the 960-ft Olympia Tower for a view of the city and the Alps; there's also a revolving restaurant near the top. Take the U-bahn 3 to the park. ☎ *089/306–72414, 089/306–72818 restaurant.* 🎟 *Main stadium DM 1, tower elevator DM 5. Stadium DM 2.50. Tours (Apr.–Nov.): grand tour, starting 2 PM, DM 13; stadium tour, starting 11 AM, DM 8.* ☉ *Main stadium daily 9–4:30, tower daily 9 AM–midnight.*

Schloss Blutenburg (Blutenburg Palace). Beyond Nymphenburg, on the northwest edge of Munich, lies this medieval palace, now the home of an international collection of 500,000 children's books in more than 100 languages. Alongside this library are collections of original manuscripts, illustrations, and posters. The castle chapel, built in 1488 by Duke Sigismund, has some fine 15th-century stained glass. Take any S-bahn train to Pasing station, then Bus 73 or 76 to the castle gate. ✉ *Blutenberg 35,* ☎ *089/811–3132.* 🎟 *Free.* ☉ *Weekdays 10–5.*

★ **Schloss Nymphenburg** (Nymphenburg Palace). The major attraction away from downtown Munich is this glorious Baroque and rococo palace in the northwest suburb that was a summer home to five generations of Bavarian royalty. Nymphenburg is the largest palace of its kind in Germany, stretching more than a half mile from one wing to the other. The palace grew in size and scope over a period of more than 200 years, beginning as a summer residence built on land given by Prince Ferdinand Maria to his beloved wife, Henriette Adelaide, on the occasion of the birth of their son and heir, Max Emanuel, in 1663. She had the Theatinerkirche built as a personal expression of thanks for the birth. The Italian architect Agostino Barelli was brought from Bologna to build the palace. It was completed in 1675 by his successor, Enrico Zuccalli. Within that original building, now the central axis of the palace complex, is a magnificent hall, the Steinerner Saal, extending over two floors and richly decorated with stucco and swirling frescoes. In the summer, chamber-music concerts are given here. The decoration of the Steinerner Saal spills over into the surrounding royal chambers, one of which houses the famous **Schönheitsgalerie** (Gallery of Beauties). The walls are hung from floor to ceiling with portraits of women who caught the roving eye of Ludwig I, among them a butcher's daughter and an English duchess. The most famous portrait is of Lola Montez, a sultry beauty and high-class courtesan who, after a time as the mistress of Franz Liszt and later Alexandre Dumas, captivated Ludwig I to such an extent that he gave up his throne for her.

The palace is set in a fine park, laid out in formal French style, with low hedges and gravel walks extending into woodland. Tucked away among the ancient trees are three fascinating structures built as Nymphenburg expanded and changed occupants. Don't miss the **Amalienburg** hunting lodge, a rococo gem built by François Cuvilliés, architect of the Residenztheater. The silver-and-blue stucco of the little Amalienburg creates an atmosphere of courtly high life, making clear that the pleasures of the chase here did not always take place outdoors. In the lavishly appointed kennels you'll see that even the dogs lived in luxury. For royal tea parties another building, the **Pagodenburg,** was constructed. It has an elegant French exterior that disguises a suitably Asian interior in which exotic teas from India and China were served. Swimming parties were held in the **Badenburg,** Europe's first post-Roman heated pool.

Nymphenburg contains so much of interest that a day hardly provides enough time. Don't leave without visiting the former royal stables, the **Marstallmuseum,** or Museum of Royal Carriages. It houses a fleet of vehicles, including an elaborately decorated sleigh in which King Ludwig II once glided through the Bavarian twilight, postilion torches lighting the way. On the floor above are fine examples of Nymphenburg porcelain, produced here between 1747 and the 1920s.

A newly opened museum in the north wing of the palace has nothing to do with the Wittelsbachs but nevertheless has become one of Nymphenburg's major attractions. The ○ **Museum Mensch und Natur** (Museum of Man and Nature) concentrates on three areas of interest: the history of man, the variety of life on Earth, and man's place in the environment. Main exhibits include a huge representation of the human brain and a chunk of Alpine crystal weighing a half ton.

To reach Schloss Nymphenburg, take the U-bahn 1 from the Hauptbahnhof to Rotkreuzplatz, then pick up Tram 12, heading for Amalienburg. ☎ *089/179–080.* ✉ *Schloss Nymphenburg complex (Gesamtkarte, or combined ticket) DM 8; palace, Schönheitsgalerie, DM 4; Marstallmuseum DM 3.* ○ *Apr.–Sept., daily 9–12:30 and 1:30–5; Oct.–Mar., daily 10–12:30 and 1:30–4.* ✉ *Museum Mensch und Natur DM 3, free Sun.* ○ *Tues.–Sun. 9–5. All except Amalienburg and gardens closed Mon.*

Schloss Schleissheim (Schleissheim Palace). In 1597 Duke Wilhelm V decided to look for a peaceful retreat outside Munich and found what he wanted at this palace, then far beyond the city walls but now only a short ride on a train and a bus. A later ruler, Prince Max Emanuel, extended the palace and added a second, smaller one, the Lustheim. Separated from the main palace by a formal garden and a decorative canal, the Lustheim houses Germany's largest collection of Meissen porcelain. To reach the palace, take the suburban S-bahn 1 line (to Oberschleissheim station) and then Bus 292 (which doesn't run on weekends). ✉ *Maximilianshof 1, Oberschleissheim,* ☎ *089/315–5272.* ✉ *Combined ticket for palaces and porcelain collection DM 5.* ○ *Tues.–Sun. 10–12:30 and 1:30–5.*

Südfriedhof (Southern Cemetery). At this museum-piece cemetery, you'll find many famous names but few tourists. Four hundred years ago it was a graveyard beyond the city walls for plague victims and paupers. During the 19th century it was refashioned into an upscale last resting place by the city architect Friedrich von Gärtner. Royal architect Leo von Klenze designed some of the headstones, and both he and von Gärtner are among the famous names you'll find there. The last burial here took place more than 40 years ago. The Südfriedhof is a short 10-minute walk south from the U-bahn station at Sendlinger-Tor-Platz. ⊠ *Thalkirchnerstr.*

3 Dining

MUNICH RATES AS Germany's gourmet capital, and it has an inordinate number of high-class French restaurants, some with chef-owners who honed their skills under such Gallic masters as Paul Bocuse. For connoisseurs, wining and dining at Tantris or the Königshof could well turn into the equivalent of a religious experience; culinary creations are accorded the status of works of art on a par with a Bach fugue or Dürer painting, with tabs worthy of a king's ransom. Epicureans are convinced that one can dine as well in Munich as in any other city on the Continent, including Paris, Brussels, and Rome, and perhaps it's true. It certainly is in a number of the top-rated restaurants listed below.

However, for many the true glory of Munich's kitchen artistry is to be experienced in those rustically decorated, traditional eating places that serve down-home Bavarian specialties in ample portions. The city's renowned beer and wine restaurants offer superb atmosphere, low prices, and as much wholesome German food as you'll ever want. They're open at just about any hour of the day or night—you can order your roast pork at 11 AM or 11 PM.

CATEGORY	COST*
$$$$	over DM 95
$$$	DM 65–DM 95
$$	DM 45–DM 65
$	under DM 45

per person for a three-course meal, excluding drinks

Budget Eating Tips

Butcher shops, known as *Metzgerei,* often have a corner that serves warm snacks. The Vinzenz-Murr chain in Munich and Bavaria has particularly good-value food. Try *Warmer Leberkäs mit Kartoffelsalat,* a typical Bavarian specialty, which is a sort of baked meat loaf with sweet mustard and potato salad.

For lunch, restaurants in local **department stores** (*Kaufhäuser*) are especially recommended for wholesome, appetizing, and inexpensive food. Kaufhof, Karstadt, and Hertie are names to note.

Often located in pedestrian zones, *Imbiss* **snack stands** can be found in almost every busy shopping street, in parking lots, train stations, and near markets. They serve *Würste* (sausages), grilled, roasted, or boiled, of every shape and size, and rolls filled with cheese, cold meat, or fish. Prices range from DM 3 to DM 6 per portion.

Munich Restaurants

$$$$ ✕ **Königshof.** The view here is great inside and out—ask for a panoramic window table overlooking Karlsplatz—in what is probably Munich's most exquisitely decorated restaurant. The service is of equally high standard. French nouvelle cuisine dominates. ⊠ *Karlspl. 25,* ☎ *089/551–36142. Reservations essential. Jacket and tie. AE, DC, MC, V.*

$$$$ ✕ **Tantris.** Chef Hans Haas has kept this restaurant with a
★ modernist look among the top five dining establishments in Munich, and in 1994 Germany's premier food critics voted him the country's top chef. You, too, will be impressed by the exotic nouvelle cuisine on the menu, including such specialties as shellfish and creamed potato soup and roasted wood pigeon with scented rice. But you may wish to ignore the bare concrete surroundings and the garish orange-and-yellow decor. ⊠ *Johann-Fichter-Str. 7,* ☎ *089/362–061. Reservations essential. Jacket and tie. AE, DC, MC, V. Closed Sun.*

$$$ ✕ **Bistro Terrine.** Tucked away self-effacingly in a corner of a Schwabing shopping arcade, the bistro is one of this lively area's most charming upmarket restaurants. Crisp blue-and-white linen, cane-back chairs, and art-nouveau lamps give it a French atmosphere matched by the excellent Gallic-influenced menu. A cozy aperitif bar completes the harmonious picture. ⊠ *Amalienstr. 89,* ☎ *089/281–780. AE, DC, MC, V. Closed Sun. No lunch Mon.*

$$$ ✕ **Dukatz.** Join the literary crowd at Munich's latest "in"
★ scene—the high-vaulted bar and restaurant in the new "House of Literature." The English-language press can be found among the heap of newspapers that is at the disposal of customers who settle for coffee in the airy café that fronts the restaurant. Here, tables buzz with talk of publishing deals and problem authors. Food is predominantly "nouvelle German," with traditional dishes such as calves' head and lamb's tripe offered with a light, almost Gallic touch. ⊠ *Salvatorplatz 1,* ☎ *089/291–9600. No credit cards.*

42

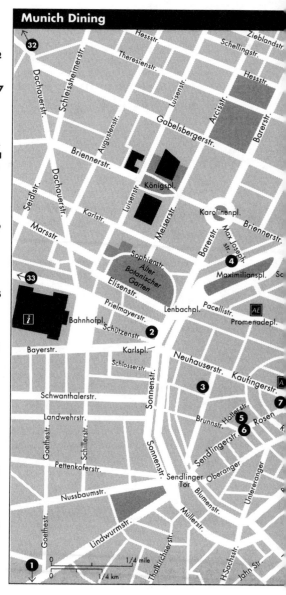

Munich Dining

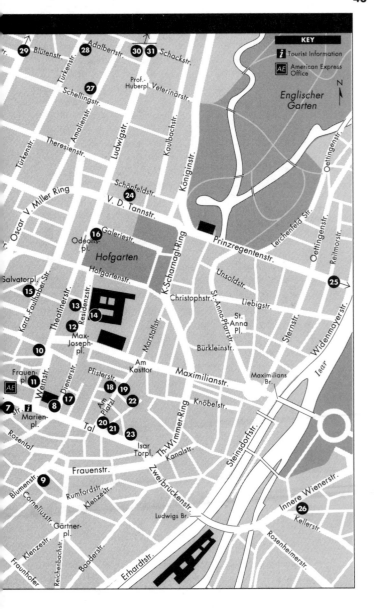

KEY

i Tourist Information

Ae American Express Office

N

Englischer Garten

Blütenstr. ㉙

Adalbertstr. ㉘

Schackstr. ㉚ ㉛

Türkenstr.

Prof.-Huberpl. Veterinärstr.

Schellingstr. ㉗

Amalienstr.

Ludwigstr.

Kaulbachstr.

Königinstr.

Oettingenstr.

Türkenstr.

Theresienstr.

r. Oscar V. Miller Ring

Schönfeldstr. ㉔

V. D. Tannstr.

Prinzregentenstr.

Lerchenfeld Str.

Oettingenstr.

Reitmorstr.

Galeriestr. ㉚

Odeons pl. ㉖

Hofgarten

K-Scharnagl-Ring

Unsoldstr.

Widenmayerstr.

Salvatorpl. ㉕

Hofgartenstr.

Christophstr.

St.-Anna-Pfarrstr.

Liebigstr.

St. Anna Pl.

Siemensstr.

Isar

Kard.-Faulhaber-Str. ㉕

Theatinerstr.

Residenzstr. ㉓

㉔

Marstallstr.

Bürkleinstr.

㉒

㉑

Max-Joseph-pl.

㉒

Am Kosttor

Maximilianstr.

Maximilians Br.

Frauen-pl. Ae ㉑

Weinstr.

Dienerstr.

Pfisterstr.

㉘ ㉙

Knöbelstr.

㉗

㉒

㉖

Steinsdorfstr.

㉔ ㉑ ㉒

Am Platzl

Tal

㉓

㉞

Marien-pl. *i*

Str.

Isar Torpl.

Kanalstr.

Rosental

Frauenstr.

Th-Wimmer-Ring

Blumenstr.

㉙

Rumfordstr.

Klenzestr.

Zweibrückenstr.

Innere Wienerstr.

Corneliusstr.

Gärtner-pl.

Ludwigs Br.

㉖

Kellerstr.

Klenzestr.

Reichenbachstr.

Baaderstr.

Fraunhofer

Erhardtstr.

Rosenheimerstr.

$$$ ✕ **Käfers am Odeonsplatz.** This smart restaurant and even
★ smarter piano bar is Michael Käfer's latest addition to his
impressive collection of nightspots; it meets the exacting
standards he sets for himself and his team. Spotless white linen
and the finest crystal set the tone of a restaurant that looks
out onto elegant Odeonsplatz. The accent is on fish, with fine
Scottish salmon sharing menu space with imaginative cre-
ations like house-made ravioli stuffed with lobster. Before or
after the meal, a stop at the busy bar is recommended, par-
ticularly if the concert grand piano is in use (and especially
if one of the regular American guest pianists is at the key-
board). ⌧ *Odeonspl. 3,* ☎ *089/290–7530. AE, MC, V.*

$$$ ✕ **Käferschänke.** Fresh seafood, imported daily from the
south of France, is the attraction here. Try the grilled
prawns in a sweet-and-sour sauce. The rustic decor, com-
plemented by some fine antiques, is sure to delight no mat-
ter what you order. The restaurant is in the upscale
Bogenhausen suburb, a 10-minute taxi ride from downtown.
⌧ *Schumannstr. 1,* ☎ *089/4168–247. Jacket and tie. AE,
DC, MC. Closed Sun.*

$$$ ✕ **Preysing Keller.** Devotees of all that's best in modern Ger-
man cooking—food that's light and sophisticated but with
recognizably Teutonic touches—will love the Preysing Keller.
It's in a 16th-century cellar, though it has been so overrestored
there's practically no indication of its age or original char-
acter. Never mind—it's the food, the extensive wine list, and
the perfect service that make this restaurant special. ⌧ *In-
nere-Wiener-Str. 6,* ☎ *089/4584–5260. Reservations es-
sential. Jacket and tie. No credit cards. Closed Sun.*

$$ ✕ **Austernkeller.** *Austern* (Oysters) are the specialty of this
cellar restaurant, although many other varieties of seafood—
all flown in daily from France—help fill its imaginative menu.
The lobster thermidor is expensive (DM 46) but surpasses
that served elsewhere in Munich, while a rich fish soup can
be ordered for less than DM 10. The fussy, fishnet-hung
decor is a shade too maritime, especially for downtown Munich, but the starched white linen and glittering glassware
and cutlery add a note of elegance. ⌧ *Stollbergstr. 11,* ☎
089/298–787. MC. Closed lunch.

$$ ✕ **Bamberger Haus.** The faded elegance of this historic old
house on the edge of Schwabing's Luitpold Park disguises
an up-to-date kitchen, which conjures up inexpensive dishes

of modern flair and imagination. Vegetarians are well catered to with cheap and filling vegetable gratins. The cellar beer tavern was reopened in 1996 after extensive renovations and serves one of the best ales in town. In summer reserve a table on the terrace and eat under shady chestnut trees with a view of the park. ⊠ *Brunnerstr. 2,* ☎ *089/ 308–8966. AE, MC, V.*

$$ ✗ **Franziskaner.** Vaulted archways, cavernous rooms interspersed with intimate dining areas, bold blue frescoes, long wood tables, and a sort of spic-and-span medieval atmosphere—the look without the dirt—set the mood. This is the place for an early morning *Weisswurst* and a beer; Bavarians swear it will banish all trace of that morning-after feeling. The Franziskaner is right by the State Opera. ⊠ *Perusastr. 5,* ☎ *089/231–8120. Reservations not accepted. AE, DC, MC, V.*

$$ ✗ **Glockenbach.** This small, highly popular restaurant with dark-wood paneling inside serves mostly fish entrées, prepared by the acclaimed chef and owner, Karl Ederer. Book ahead to enjoy such specialties as freshwater fish ragout from the Starnberger Lake. Highlights of the meat menu are Bavarian Forest lamb and free-range chicken with wild mushrooms. ⊠ *Kapuzinerstr. 29,* ☎ *089/534–043. Reservations essential. AE, MC, V. Closed Sun. and Mon.*

$$ ✗ **Halali.** The Halali is an old-style Munich restaurant—polished wood paneling and antlers on the walls—that offers new-style regional specialties, such as venison in juniper-berry sauce and marinated beef on a bean salad. Save room for the homemade vanilla ice cream. ⊠ *Schönfeldstr. 22,* ☎ *089/ 285–909. Jacket and tie. AE, MC, V. Closed Sun.*

$$ ✗ **Hunsingers Pacific.** Werner Hunsinger, one of Germany's top restaurateurs, has taken over the premises of the former Aubergine on fashionable Maximiliansplatz and has turned it into a reasonably priced restaurant serving food from the Pacific Rim, an eclectic culinary region bordered by East Asia, Australia, and North and South America. The restaurant's clam chowder is the most authentic to be found in the city, while another praised specialty is the Chilean-style filet steak, wrapped in a mantle of onion and aubergine-flavored maize. Lunchtime two-course meals cost less than DM 20 and evening meals cost between DM 45 and DM

55. ⊠ Maximilianspl. 5, ☎ 089/550–29741. MC, V. No lunch weekends.

$$ ✗ **Ratskeller.** Munich's Ratskeller is one of the few city-hall cellar restaurants to offer vegetarian dishes alongside the normal array of hearty and filling traditional fare. If turnip in cheese sauce is on the menu, you won't need to be a vegetarian to appreciate it. The decor is much as you would expect, with vaulted stone ceilings and flickering candles. ⊠ *Marienpl. 8, ☎ 089/220–313. AE, MC, V.*

$$ ✗ **Spatenhaus.** A view of the opera house and the royal palace
★ complements the Bavarian mood of the wood-paneled and beamed Spatenhaus. The menu is international, however, with more or less everything from artichokes to *zuppa Romana* (alcohol-soaked, fruity Italian cake-pudding). But since you're in Bavaria, why not do as the Bavarians do? Try the Bavarian Plate, an enormous mixture of local meats and sausages. ⊠ *Residenzstr. 12, ☎ 089/290–7060. DC, MC, V.*

$$ ✗ **Spöckmeier.** This rambling, solidly Bavarian beer restaurant spread over three floors, including a snug *Keller* (cellar), is famous for its homemade Weisswurst. If you've just stopped in for a snack and don't fancy the fat breakfast sausage, order coffee and pretzels or, in the afternoon, a wedge of cheesecake. The daily changing menu also offers more than two dozen hearty main-course dishes and a choice of four draft beers. The house *Eintopf* (a rich broth of noodles and pork) is a meal in itself. The Spöckmeier is only 50 yards from Marienplatz; on sunny summer days tables are set outside in the auto-free street. ⊠ *Rosenstr. 9, ☎ 089/268–088. AE, DC, MC, V.*

$$ ✗ **Weichandhof.** This rambling old farmhouse-style restaurant is on the northwestern outskirts of town, in the leafy residential suburb of Obermenzing and near the start of the Stuttgart Autobahn. If you're heading that way, a stop here is strongly recommended, but even a special trip from the city center is worthwhile. The food is excellent, with a menu based on traditional Bavarian and regional German and Austrian fare; roast suckling pig, pork knuckle, and Vienna-style boiled beef are basic staples. In summer or on warm spring and autumn evenings the vine-clad terrace beckons. In winter tiled stoves give a warm glow to the wood-paneled dining rooms. ⊠ *Betzenweg 81, ☎ 089/891–1600 or 089/811–1621. MC. Closed weekends.*

$$ ✕ **Welser Kuche.** It's less a question of what you eat at this medieval-style cellar restaurant than how you eat it—with your fingers and a hunting knife, in the manner of 16th-century baronial banquets. You're welcomed by pretty "serving wenches" who tie a protective bib around your neck, proffer a hunting horn of mead, and show you to one of the oak trestle tables that complete the authentic-looking surroundings. It's best to go in a group, but room will always be found for couples or those dining alone. The full menu runs to 10 dishes, although you can settle for less and choose à la carte. ⊠ *Residenzstr. 2,* ☎ *089/296–565. MC. No lunch.*

$$ ✕ **Wirtshaus im Weinstadl.** Tucked away at the end of a small alley off a busy shopping street and overlooked by most passersby, the historic Weinstadl is well worth hunting out. In summer the courtyard beer garden is a cool delight, with a humorous fountain depicting a Munich burgher quaffing a glass of wine; the fountain splashes away beneath original Renaissance galleries. In winter the brass-studded oaken door opens onto a vaulted dining room where traditional Bavarian fare is served at bench-lined tables. A lunchtime menu and a glass of excellent beer leave change from DM 20. The equally atmospheric cellar, reached via a winding staircase, features live music on Friday and Saturday evenings. ⊠ *Burgstr. 5,* ☎ *089/290–4044. AE, DC, MC.*

$ ✕ **Altes Hackerhaus.** Since 1570 beer has been brewed or served here, the birthplace of Hacher-Pschorr, a still-active Munich brewery. Today the site is a cozy, upscale restaurant with three floors of wood-paneled rooms. In summer you can order a cheese plate and beer in the cool, flower-decorated inner courtyard; in winter you can snuggle in a corner of the Ratsstube and warm up on thick homemade potato broth, followed by schnitzel and *Bratkartoffein* (pan-fried potatoes). ⊠ *Sendlinger-Str. 75,* ☎ *089/260–5026. AE, DC, MC, V.*

$ ✕ **Augustiner Keller.** This 19th-century establishment is the flagship beer restaurant of one of Munich's oldest breweries, Augustiner. The decor emphasizes wood—from the refurbished parquet floors to the wood barrels from which the beer is drawn. The menu changes daily and offers a full range of Bavarian specialties, but try to order *Teller-fleisch*—cold roast beef with lashings of horseradish, served on a big wood board. Follow that with *Dampfnudeln* (suet pudding served with custard) and you won't feel hungry again for 24 hours. The communal atmosphere of the two baronial hall-like rooms makes this a better place for meeting locals than for attempting a quiet meal for two. ✉ *Arnulfstr. 52*, ☎ *089/594–393. AE, DC, MC, V.*

$ ✗ **Brauhaus zum Brez'n.** This hostelry is bedecked in the blue-and-white-check colors of the Bavarian flag. The eating and drinking are spread over three floors and cater to a broad clientele—from local business lunchers to hungry night owls emerging from Schwabing's bars and looking for a bite at 2 AM. Brez'n offers a big all-day menu of traditional roasts, to be washed down with a choice of three draft beers. ✉ *Leopoldstr. 72*, ☎ *089/390–092. No credit cards.*

$ ✗ **Dürnbräu.** A fountain plays outside this picturesque old Bavarian inn. Inside, it's crowded and noisy. Expect to share a table; your fellow diners will range from businesspeople to students. The food is resolutely traditional. Try the cream of spinach soup and the boiled beef. ✉ *Dürnbräugasse 2*, ☎ *089/222–195. AE, DC, MC, V.*

$ ✗ **Erstes Münchner Kartoffelhaus.** When potatoes were first introduced to Germany, they were dismissed as fodder fit only for animals or the very lowest strata of society. Frederick the Great was largely responsible for putting them on the dining tables of even the nobility, and now the lowly potato is an indispensable part of the German diet. In "Munich's first potato house" they come in all forms, from the simplest baked potato with sour cream to gratin creations with shrimps and salmon. This restaurant is great fun and a great value, too. ✉ *Hochbrückenstr. 3*, ☎ *089/ 296–331. AE, MC, V. Closed Sun.*

$ ✗ **Grüne Gans.** This small, chummy restaurant near Viktualienmarkt is popular with local entertainers, whose photographs clutter the walls. International fare with regional German influences dominates the menu, although there are a few Chinese dishes. Try the chervil cream soup, followed by calves' kidneys in tarragon sauce. ✉ *Am Einlass 5*, ☎ *089/266–228. Reservations essential. No credit cards. Closed Sun. No lunch.*

$ ✗ **Haxnbauer.** This is one of Munich's more sophisticated beer restaurants. There's the usual series of interlinking rooms—some large, some small—and the usual sturdy yet pretty Bavarian decoration. But there is a much greater emphasis on the food here than in similar places. Try the *Schweineshaxn* (pork shanks) cooked over a charcoal fire. ⊠ *Münzstr. 2,* ☎ *089/221–922. MC, V.*

$ ✕ **Hofbräuhaus.** The sound of the constantly playing oompah band draws passersby into this father of all beer halls, in which trumpet, drum, and accordion music blends with singing and shouting drinkers to produce an earsplitting din. This is no place for the fainthearted, although a trip to Munich would be incomplete without a visit to the Hofbräuhaus. Upstairs is a more peaceful restaurant. In March, May, and September ask for one of the special, extra-strong seasonal beers (Starkbier, Maibock, Märzen), which complement the heavy, traditional Bavarian fare. ⊠ *Am Platzl,* ☎ *089/221–676. Reservations not accepted. MC, V.*

$ ✕ **Hundskugel.** This is Munich's oldest tavern, dating from
★ 1440; history positively drips from its crooked walls. The food is surprisingly good. If *Spanferkel*—roast suckling pig—is on the menu, make a point of ordering it. This is simple Bavarian fare at its best. ⊠ *Hotterstr. 18,* ☎ *089/ 264–272. No credit cards.*

$ ✕ **Max-Emanuel-Brauerei.** This historic old brewery tavern is a great value, with hearty Bavarian dishes rarely costing more than DM 20; at lunchtime that easily covers the cost of an all-you-can-eat buffet. The main dining room has a stage, so the bill often includes a cabaret or jazz concert. In summer take a table outside in the secluded little beer garden. ⊠ *Adalbertstr. 33,* ☎ *089/271–5158. AE, MC.*

$ ✕ **Nürnberger Bratwurst Glöckl am Dom.** Munich's most original beer tavern is dedicated to a specialty from a rival city, Nuremberg, whose delicious, finger-size sausages (Nürnberger Bratwürste) form the staple dish of the hearty menu. They're served by a busy team of friendly waitresses dressed in Bavarian dirndls, who flit between the crowded tables with remarkable agility. In summer, tables are placed outside under a bright awning and in the shade of the nearby Dom. In winter the dark-paneled, mellow dining rooms provide relief from the cold. ⊠ *Frauenpl. 9,* ☎ *089/ 220–385. No credit cards.*

$ ✕ **Pfälzer Weinprobierstube.** A warren of stone-vaulted rooms of various sizes, wood tables, flickering candles, dirndl-clad waitresses, and a vast range of wines add up to an experience as close to everyone's image of timeless Germany as you're likely to get. The wines are mostly from the Palatinate, the German *Pfalz,* as are many of the specialties on the limuted menu. Here you'll find Chancellor Kohl's favorite dish, *Saumagen* (meat loaf, spiced with herbs and cooked in a pig's stomach). ⊠ *Residenzstr. 1,* ☎ *089/225–628. Reservations not accepted. No credit cards.*

$ ✕ **Weinhaus Neuner.** Munich's oldest wine tavern serves good food as well as superior wines in its three varied nooks and crannies: the wood-paneled restaurant, the Weinstübl, and the small bistro. The choice of food is remarkable, from nouvelle German to old-fashioned country. Specialties include home-smoked beef and salmon. ⊠ *Herzogspitalstr. 8,* ☎ *089/260–3954. AE, DC, MC. Closed Sun. No lunch Sat.*

$ ✕ **Weisses Bräuhaus.** If you have developed a taste for Munich's Weissbier, this is the place to enjoy it. Other beers, including a very strong Aventinus, are available, but the accent is unmistakably on the Schneider brewery's famous specialty, the Schneiderweisse, a yeast-fermented wheat beer. It's served with hearty Bavarian fare, mostly variations of pork and dumplings or cabbage, by some of Munich's friendliest waitresses, good-humored women in crisp black dresses, who appear to match exactly the Jugendstil features of the restaurant's beautifully restored interior. ⊠ *Tal 7,* ☎ *089/299–875. No credit cards.*

4 Lodging

MAKE RESERVATIONS well in advance, and be prepared for higher-than-average rates. Though Munich has a vast number of hotels in all price ranges, many of the most popular are fully booked year-round; this is a major trade and convention city as well as a prime tourist destination. If you plan to visit during *Mode Wochen* (Fashion Weeks) in March and September or during the Oktoberfest at the end of September, make reservations at least four months in advance.

Some of the large, very expensive ($$$$) hotels that cater to expense-account business travelers have very attractive weekend discount rates—sometimes as much as 50% below normal prices. Conversely, regular rates can go up during big trade fairs. Check well in advance, either through your travel agent or directly with the hotel.

The tourist office at Rindermarkt 1, D–80331 Munich 1, has a reservations department, but it will not accept telephone reservations. There's also a reservations office at the airport. The best bet for finding a room if you arrive without a reservation is the tourist office in the main train station, on the south side abutting Bayerstrasse, which is open daily 8 AM–10 PM (no telephone bookings).

CATEGORY	COST*
$$$$	over DM 300
$$$	DM 200–DM 300
$$	DM 140–DM 200
$	under DM 140

All prices are for two people in a double room, including tax and service charge.

$$$$ 🏨 **Bayerischer Hof.** This is one of Munich's most traditional luxury hotels. It's on a ritzy shopping street, and there's a series of exclusive shops right outside the imposing marble entrance. Public rooms are decorated with antiques, fine paintings, marble, and painted wood. Old-fashioned comfort and class abound in the older rooms; some of the newer rooms are more functional. ✉ *Promenadenpl. 2–6, D–80333,* ☎ *089/21200,* 📠 *089/212–0906. 440 rooms.*

3 restaurants, pool, beauty salon, massage, sauna, night-club, parking (fee). AE, DC, MC, V.

$$$$ ⊞ **Platzl.** The Platzl has won awards and wide recognition for its ecologically aware management. It stands in the historic heart of Munich, near the famous Hofbräuhaus beer hall and a couple of minutes' walk from Marienplatz and many other landmarks. The Aying brewery owners have done the soundproof rooms in rustic Bavarian style. ⊠ *Sparkassenstr. 10, D–80331, ☎ 089/237–030; 800/448–8355 in the U.S., 🗚 089/2370–3800. 167 rooms. Restaurant, bar, sauna, steam room, exercise room, parking. AE, DC, MC, V.*

$$$$ ⊞ **Rafael.** This is indisputably Munich's most luxurious
★ hotel, with prices to match (doubles cost more than DM 500 and suites up to DM 2,000). No wonder Britain's Prince Charles chose it as his residence when visiting Munich in 1995, making a very visible break with royal tradition. The hotel occupies a beautifully renovated neo-Renaissance building that was a high-society ballroom during the late 19th century. Today it tries to recapture some of that bygone era with 24-hour service, including such personalized amenities as in-house butlers. Rooms are individually furnished and extravagantly decorated, in addition to offering many extras, including fax machines. ⊠ *Neuturmstr. 1, D–80331, ☎ 089/290–980, 🗚 089/222–539. 54 rooms, 19 suites. Restaurant, 2 bars, pool, sauna. AE, DC, MC, V.*

$$$$ ⊞ **Trustee Park Hotel.** Even the mansard rooms are spacious and airy in this newly constructed hotel on the edge of Munich's fairgrounds and Oktoberfest site. In fact the hotel claims that none of its rooms is less than 400 square ft. Suites are larger than many luxury apartments, and some of them are equipped with small kitchens. The sleek, modern rooms are mostly decorated with light woods and pastel-colored fabrics and carpeting; larger rooms and suites get a lot of light, thanks to the floor-to-ceiling windows. Families are particularly welcome, and a baby-sitting service is provided. ⊠ *Parkstr. 31, D–80339, ☎ 089/519–950, 🗚 089/519–95420. 35 rooms. Restaurant, bar. AE, DC, MC, V.*

$$$$ ⊞ **Vier Jahreszeiten Kempinski.** The Vier Jahreszeiten (Four
★ Seasons) has been playing host to the world's wealthy and

54

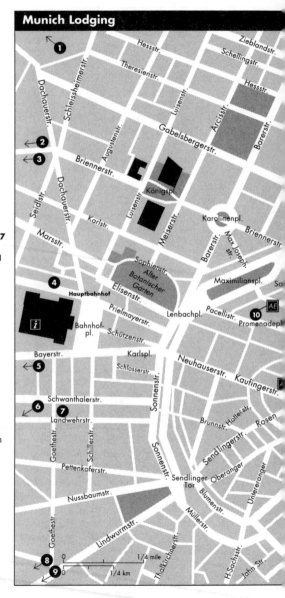

Munich Lodging

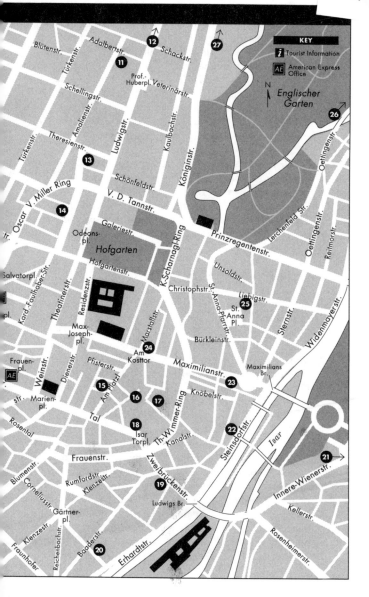

5

Englischer Garten

N

Blütenstr.
Adalbertstr.
Schackstr.
Türkenstr.
Prof.-Huberpl. Veterinärstr.
Schellingstr.
Amalienstr.
Ludwigstr.
Kaulbachstr.
Theresienstr.
Türkenstr.
Königinstr.
Oettingenstr.
Schönfeldstr.
Oscar V. Miller Ring
V. D. Tannstr.
Galeriestr.
Odéons-pl.
Hofgarten
Prinzregentenstr.
Lerchenfeld Str.
Oettingenstr.
Reitmorstr.
Hofgartenstr.
Salvatorpl.
Unsoldstr.
Kard.-Faulhaber-Str.
Theatinerstr.
Residenzstr.
Christophstr.
St.-Anna-Pfarrstr.
Liebigstr.
St.-Anna-Pl
Widenmayerstr.
Sternstr.
Max-Joseph-pl.
Marstallstr.
Bürkleinstr.
Frauen-pl.
AE
Weinstr.
Dienerstr.
Pfisterstr.
Am Kosttor
Maximilianstr.
Maximilians Br.
Marien-pl.
Am Platzl
Knöbelstr.
Tal
Th.-Wimmer-Ring
Isar
Steinsdorfstr.
Isar
Rosental
Isar Torpl.
Kanalstr.
Frauenstr.
Zweibrückenstr.
Blumenstr.
CornelIusstr.
Rumfordstr.
Klenzestr.
Innere-Wiener-str.
Gärtner-pl.
Ludwigs Br.
Kellerstr.
Klenzestr.
Reichenbachstr.
Baaderstr.
Rosenheimerstr.
Fraunhofer
Erhardtstr.

titled for more than a century. It has an unbeatable location on Maximilianstrasse, Munich's premier shopping street, only a few minutes' walk from the heart of the city. Elegance and luxury set the tone throughout; many rooms have handsome antique pieces. The main floor's restaurant is Bistro Eck, and the Theater bar/restaurant is in the cellar. ⊠ *Maximilianstr. 17, D–80539,* ☎ *089/21250, 516/794–2670 Kempinski Reservation Service,* FAX *089/212–52000. 268 rooms, 48 suites. 2 restaurants, piano bar, pool, massage, sauna, exercise room, car rental, parking. AE, DC, MC, V.*

$$$–
$$$$
🏨 **Eden Hotel Wolff.** Chandeliers and dark-wood paneling in the public rooms underline the old-fashioned elegance of this downtown favorite. It's directly across the street from the train station and near the Theresienwiese fairgrounds. The rooms are comfortable, and most are spacious. You can dine on excellent Bavarian specialties in the intimate Zirbelstube restaurant. ⊠ *Arnulfstr. 4, D–80335,* ☎ *089/551–150,* FAX *089/551–15555. 209 rooms, 2 suites. Restaurant, bar, café, parking (fee). AE, DC, MC, V.*

$$$–
$$$$
🏨 **Torbräu.** You'll sleep under the shadow of one of Munich's ancient city gates—the 14th-century Isartor—if you stay here. This snug hotel offers comfortable rooms decorated in plush and ornate Italian style and an excellent location midway between the Marienplatz and the Deutsches Museum (and around the corner from the Hofbräuhaus). The Torbräu has a moderately priced Italian restaurant, the Firenze, and a good café tucked away in a corner of the arcaded facade. ⊠ *Tal 41, D–80331,* ☎ *089/225–016,* FAX *089/225–019. 83 rooms, 3 suites. Restaurant, café, bowling. AE, MC, V.*

$$$
★
🏨 **Admiral.** Although it's in the heart of the city, close to the Isar River and Deutsches Museum, the small, privately owned Admiral enjoys a quiet side-street location and its own garden. Many of the cozily furnished and warmly decorated bedrooms have a balcony overlooking the garden. Bowls of fresh fruit are part of the friendly welcome awaiting guests. The breakfast buffet is a dream, complete with homemade jams, in-season strawberries, and Italian and French delicacies. ⊠ *Kohlstr. 9, D–80469,* ☎ *089/226–641,* FAX *089/216350. 33 rooms. Bar, parking. AE, DC, MC, V.*

$$$ 🏨 **Advokat.** Owner Kevin Voigt designed much of the furniture of his exquisite new hotel and had it made by Italian craftsmen. The Italian touch is everywhere, from the sleek, minimalist lines of the bedroom furniture and fittings to the choice prints and modern Florentine mirrors on the walls. If you value modern taste over plush "luxury" this is the hotel for you. ⊠ *Baaderstr. 1, D–80469,* ☎ *089/216–310,* 🖷 *089/216–3190. 50 rooms. AE, DC, MC, V.*

$$$ 🏨 **Arabella Airport.** This first-class lodging is only five minutes from the new Franz Josef Strauss Airport, and the hotel operates a courtesy shuttle bus. Built primarily to cater to businesspeople (there are numerous conference rooms), the Arabella has plenty of leisure facilities and is ideal for any traveler who has an early morning departure or a late-evening arrival flight. The three-story, Bavarian rustic-style building is surrounded by greenery. Rooms are furnished in light pinewood, with Laura Ashley fabrics. ⊠ *Freisingerstr. 80, D–85445 Schwaig,* ☎ *089/9272–2750,* 🖷 *089/9272–2800. 162 rooms, 8 suites. 2 restaurants, bar, indoor pool, sauna, steam room, exercise room. AE, DC, MC, V.*

$$$ 🏨 **Erzgiesserei Europe.** Its location on a dull little street in an uninteresting section of the city is this hotel's only drawback, but even that is easily overcome—the nearby subway whisks you in five minutes to central Karlsplatz, convenient to the pedestrian shopping area and the main railway station. Rooms in this attractive hotel are particularly bright, decorated in soft pastels with good reproductions on the walls. The cobblestone garden café is a haven of peace. ⊠ *Erzgiessereistr. 15, D–80335,* ☎ *089/126–820,* 🖷 *089/123–6198. 105 rooms, 1 suite. Restaurant, bar, café, parking. AE, DC, MC, V.*

$$$ 🏨 **Hotel Concorde.** The centrally located Concorde wants to do its bit toward relieving traffic congestion, so guests who arrive from the airport on the S-bahn can exchange their ticket at the reception desk for a welcome champagne or cocktail. With the nearest S-bahn station (Isartor) only a two-minute walk away, why not take the hotel up on its offer? Rooms are decorated in pastel tones and light woods, with modern prints on the walls. The hotel has no restaurant, but a large breakfast buffet is served in its stylish, mirrored Salon Margarita. ⊠ *Herrnstr. 38, D–80539,* ☎ *089/*

224–515, FAX 089/228–3282. *67 rooms, 4 suites. Lounge. AE, DC, MC, V.*

$$$ ☎ **Pannonia Hotel Königin Elisabeth.** A bright, modern interior, with emphasis on the color pink, lies behind the protected neoclassical facade of this Pannonia-group hotel, opened in 1990 and a 15-minute tram ride northwest of the city center. Children under 12 stay free in their parents' room. ✉ *Leonrodstr. 79, D–80636,* ☎ *089/126–860,* FAX *089/1268–6459. 79 rooms. Restaurant, bar, beer garden, hot tub, sauna, steam room, exercise room. AE, DC, MC, V.*

$$$ ☎ **Splendid.** Chandelier-hung public rooms, complete with
★ Louis XVI–era antiques and Oriental rugs, give this small hotel something of the atmosphere of a spaciously grand 19th-century city residence. Have breakfast in the small courtyard in summer. There's no restaurant, but the bar serves snacks as well as drinks. The chic shops of the Maximilianstrasse are a five-minute stroll away. ✉ *Maximilianstr. 54, D–80538,* ☎ *089/296–606,* FAX *089/291–3176. 32 rooms, 7 suites. Bar. AE, DC, MC, V.*

$$–$$$ ☎ **Adria.** This modern, comfortable hotel is ideally located in the upmarket area of Lehel, in the middle of Munich's museum quarter. Rooms are large and tastefully decorated, with old prints on the pale-pink walls, Oriental rugs on the floors, and flowers beside the double beds. More than half the rooms were fully renovated in 1997. A spectacular breakfast buffet (including a glass of sparkling wine) is included in the room rate. There's no hotel restaurant, but the area is rich in good restaurants, bistros, and bars. ✉ *Liebigstr. 8a, D–80538,* ☎ *089/293–081,* FAX *089/227–015. 46 rooms, 43 with bath. AE, MC, V.*

$$–$$$ ☎ **Brack.** Oktoberfest visitors value the Brack's proximity to the beer festival grounds, and its location—on a busy, tree-lined thoroughfare just south of the center—is handy for other city attractions. Rooms are furnished in light, friendly veneers and are soundproof (a particularly useful feature during the Oktoberfest). The Brack has no restaurant, but the buffet breakfast will set you up for the day. ✉ *Lindwurmstr. 153, D–80327,* ☎ *089/747–2550,* FAX *089/747–25599. 50 rooms. AE, DC, MC, V.*

$$ ☎ **Bauer.** Head here for a good-value Bavarian-rustic inn that provides country comforts (painted wardrobes, raw light pine, lots of blue-and-white-check patterns) yet is within easy reach of the city. The family-run Bauer, 10 km (6 mi) from the city center, is best for those traveling by car, although the S-bahn train line S-3 is nearby. ⊠ *Münchnerstr. 6, D–85622 Feldkirchen,* ☎ *089/90980,* FAX *089/ 909–8414. 103 rooms. Restaurant, café, indoor pool, sauna. AE, DC, MC, V.*

$$ 🏨 **Carlton.** This is a favorite of many diplomats: a small, elegant, discreet hotel on a quiet side street in the best area of downtown Munich. The American and British consulates are a short walk away, and so are some of the liveliest Schwabing bars and restaurants. Art galleries, museums, and cinemas are also in the immediate area. Rooms are on the small side, but there are four apartments with cooking facilities. ⊠ *Fürstenstr. 12, D–80333,* ☎ *089/282–061,* FAX *089/284–391. 49 rooms, 4 apartments. AE, DC, MC, V.*

$$ 🏨 **Gästehaus am Englischen Garten.** Reserve well in ad-
★ vance for a room at this popular converted water mill, over 200 years old, adjoining the Englischer Garten. The hotel, complete with ivy-clad walls and shutter-framed windows, is only a five-minute walk from the bars and shops of Schwabing. There's no restaurant, but who needs one with Schwabing's numerous eating possibilities so close? Be sure to ask for one of the 12 nostalgically old-fashioned rooms in the main building; the modern annex down the road is cheaper but lacks charm. In summer breakfast is served on the terrace. Part of the hotel's garden is an island in the old mill race. ⊠ *Liebergesellstr. 8, D–80802,* ☎ *089/ 383–9410,* FAX *089/383–94133. 27 rooms, 21 with bath or shower. No credit cards.*

$$ 🏨 **Jagdschloss.** Once a 100-year-old hunting lodge, Jagdschloss has been totally renovated and turned into a delightful hotel, on the western edge of Munich. Much of the original wood paneling has been kept, and in the hotel's beamed restaurant you'll be served Bavarian specialties by a staff dressed in traditional lederhosen (shorts in summer, breeches in winter)—just the dress for the hotel's own, sheltered beer garden. ⊠ *Alte Alle, München-Obermenzing, D–81245,* ☎ *089/820–820,* FAX *089/820–82100. 22 rooms, 1 suite. Restaurant, beer garden, playground, free parking. MC, V.*

$$ 🏨 **Mayer.** If you are willing to sacrifice a convenient location for good value, head for this family-run hotel 25 minutes by suburban train from the Hauptbahnhof. The Mayer's first-class comforts and facilities cost about half of what you'd pay at similar lodgings in town. Built in the 1970s, it is furnished in Bavarian country-rustic style—lots of pine and green and red, and check fabrics. The Mayer is a 10-minute walk or a short taxi ride from Germering station on the S-5 suburban line, eight stops west of the Hauptbahnhof. ⊠ *Augsburgerstr. 15, D–82110 Germering,* ☎ *089/844–07173,* ⅢX *089/844–094. 56 rooms. Restaurant, indoor pool. AE, MC.*

\$\$ ⊞ **Tele-Hotel.** This modern, well-appointed hotel on the out-
★ skirts of Munich is handy to the television studios at Unterföhring (hence the name) and is also conveniently located on the airport S-bahn Line 8, a 15-minute ride from downtown. Television people escape their drab canteen fare by popping into the hotel's Bavarian Hackerbräu restaurant, where a lunchtime menu for less than DM 30 is a favorite. Rooms are stylishly furnished in cherry wood. ⊠ *Bahnhofstr. 15, D–85774 Unterföhring,* ☎ *089/950–146,* ⅢX *089/950–6652. 58 rooms, 1 suite. Restaurant, bar, bowling, parking. AE, DC, MC, V.*

\$–\$\$ ⊞ **Kriemhild.** If you're traveling with children, you'll appreciate this welcoming, family-run pension in the western suburb of Nymphenburg. It's a 10-minute walk from the palace itself and around the corner from the Hirschgarten Park, site of one of the city's best beer gardens. The tram ride (No. 17) from downtown is 10 minutes. There's no restaurant. ⊠ *Guntherstr. 16, D–80639,* ☎ *089/170–077,* ⅢX *089/177–478. 18 rooms, 14 with bath. Bar. MC, V.*

\$ ⊞ **Fürst.** On a quiet street just off Odeonsplatz, on the edge
★ of the university quarter, this very basic, clean guest house is constantly busy with families and students traveling on a budget. Book early. ⊠ *Kardinal-Döpfner Str. 8, D–80333,* ☎ *089/281–043,* ⅢX *089/280–860. 19 rooms, 12 with bath. No credit cards.*

\$ ⊞ **Hotel Mirabell.** This family-run hotel reports that it has
★ "many tourists from the USA." They like its friendly atmosphere, central location (between the main railway station and the Oktoberfest fairgrounds), and its very reasonable room rates. Three apartments were added in 1998 for small groups or families. All rooms have TVs and phones, and are furnished in modern, light woods and bright prints.

The restaurant serves breakfast only, but snacks can be ordered at the bar. ✉ *Landwehrstr. 42 (entrance on Goethestr.), D–80336,* ☎ *089/549–1740,* 🖷 *089/550–3701. 65 rooms, 3 apartments. AE, MC, V.*

$ 🏨 **Hotel Pension Am Siegestor.** You ride an ancient, wood-
★ paneled, glass-door elevator up an open shaft to the fourth floor reception desk of this modest but very appealing pension, which takes up three floors of a fin-de-siècle mansion between the Siegestor monument on Leopoldstrasse and the University. Most of the simply but comfortably furnished rooms face the impressive Arts Academy across the street. Rooms on the fifth floor are particularly cozy, tucked up under the eaves. ✉ *Akademiestr. 5, D–80799,* ☎ *089/399–550 or 089/399–551,* 🖷 *089/343–050. No credit cards.*

$ 🏨 **Hotel-Pension Beck.** American and British guests receive
★ a particularly warm welcome from the Anglophile owner of the rambling, friendly Beck. Rooms were recently refurnished in pinewood. The pension has a prime location in the heart of fashionable Lehel (convenient to museums and the Englischer Garten). ✉ *Thierschstr. 36, D–80538,* ☎ *089/220–708 or 089/225–768,* 🖷 *089/220–925. 44 rooms, 5 with shower. No credit cards.*

5 Nightlife and the Arts

THE ARTS

Details of concerts and theater performances are listed in "Vorschau" and "Monatsprogramm," booklets available at most hotel reception desks, newsstands, and tourist offices. Some hotels will make ticket reservations. Or use one of the **ticket agencies** in the city center, such as **Max Hieber Konzertkasse** (✉ Liebfrauenstr. 1, ☎ 089/290–08014), or either of the two kiosks in the underground concourse at Marienplatz: the **Abendzeitung Schalterhalle** (✉ Sendlingerstr. 10, ☎ 089/267–024), or **Residenz Bücherstube** (concert tickets only; ✉ Residenzstr. 1, ☎ 089/220–868). There's also a special ticket agency for visitors with disabilities: **abr-Theaterkasse** (✉ Neuhauser Str. 9, ☎ 089/12040).

Concerts

Munich and music go together. Paradoxically, however, it's only since 1984 that the city has had a world-class concert hall: the Gasteig, a lavish brick complex standing high above the Isar River, east of downtown. It's the permanent home of the Munich Philharmonic Orchestra, which regularly performs in its Philharmonic Hall. The city has three other principal orchestras: the Bavarian State Orchestra, based at the National Theater; the Bavarian Radio Symphony Orchestra, which gives regular Sunday concerts at the Gasteig; and the Kurt Graunke Symphony Orchestra, which performs at the Gärtnerplatz Theater. The leading choral ensembles are the Munich Bach Choir, the Munich Motettenchor, and Musica Viva—the latter specializing in contemporary music.

Bayerischer Rundfunk (✉ Rundfunkpl. 1, ☎ 089/558–080). The box office is open Mon.–Thurs. 9–noon and 2–4, Fri. 9–noon.

Herkulessaal in der Residenz (✉ Hofgarten, ☎ 089/2906–7263). The box office opens one hour before performances.

Hochschule für Musik (✉ Arcisstr. 12, ☎ 089/559–101). Concerts featuring music students are given free of charge.

Olympiahalle (☎ 089/306–13577). This is one of Munich's major pop concert venues. The box office, at the ice stadium, is open weekdays 10–6 and Saturday 10–3.

Opera, Ballet, Operetta, and Musicals

Munich's Bavarian State Opera Company and its ballet ensemble perform at the **Nationaltheater** (also called the Bayerisches Staatsoper). The ticket office is at Maximilianstrasse 11 (☎ 089/2185–1920; ☉ weekdays 10–6, Sat. 10–1). The evening ticket office, at the Maximilianstrasse entrance to the theater, opens one hour before curtain time. At the romantic Jugendstil **Staatstheater am Gärtnerplatz** (⊠ Gärtnerpl. 3, ☎ 089/201-6767), a less ambitious but nevertheless high-quality program of opera, ballet, operetta, and musicals is presented. The ticket office is also at Maximilianstrasse 11. An evening ticket office opens at the theater one hour before performances.

Theater

Munich has scores of theaters and variety-show haunts, although most productions will be largely impenetrable if your German is shaky. A very active American company, the American Drama Group Europe, presents regular productions at the **Theater an der Leopoldstrasse** (⊠ Leopoldstr. 17, ☎ 089/380–14032 for program details). A British theater group, the Munich English Theater (MET) is at home in the **Theater im Karlshof** (⊠ Karlstr. 43, ☎ 089/596–611), a backyard theater with a friendly bar. Listed here are all the better-known theaters, as well as some of the smaller and more progressive spots. A visit to one or more will underline just why the Bavarian capital has such an enviable reputation as an artistic hot spot. Note that most theaters are closed during July and August.

Bayerisches Staatsschauspiel/Neues Residenztheater (Bavarian State Theater/New Residence Theater) (⊠ Max-Joseph-Pl., box office is at Maximilianstr. 11, ☎ 089/2185–1940). Open weekdays 10–1 and 2–6, Saturday 10–1, and one hour before the performance.

Cuvilliés-Theater/Altes Residenztheater (Old Residence Theater) (⊠ Max-Joseph-Pl.; entrance on Residenzstr.). The box office, at Maximilianstrasse 11 (☎ 089/221–1316), is open weekdays 10–1 and 2–6, Saturday 10–1, and one hour before the performance.

Deutsches Theater (⊠ Schwanthalerstr. 13, ☎ 089/5523–4444). The box office is open weekdays noon–6, Saturday 10–1:30.

Gasteig (⊠ Rosenheimerstr. 5, ☎ 089/5481–8181). This modern cultural complex includes two theaters—the Carl-Orff Saal and the Black Box—where plays in English are occasionally performed. The box office is open weekdays 10:30–6, Saturday 10–2.

Kleine Komödie, two theaters sharing a program of light comedy and farce (⊠ Bayerischer Hof Hotel, Promenadepl., ☎ 089/292–810; ⊠ Max-II-Denkmal, Maximilianstr. 27, ☎ 089/221–859). The box office at Bayerischer Hof is open Monday–Saturday 11–8, Sunday 3–8. The box office at Max-II-Denkmal is open Monday 11–7, Tuesday–Saturday 11–8, Sunday 3–8.

Münchner Kammerspiele-Schauspielhaus (⊠ Maximilianstr. 26, ☎ 089/237–21328). The box office is open weekdays 10–6, Saturday 10–1.

Prinzregententheater (⊠ Prinzregentenpl. 12, ☎ 089/218–52959). Munich's newly refurbished art nouveau theater is reputedly an audience favorite. It was built at the turn of the century to entice Wagner to Munich, but Bayreuth won his favor. The box office, at Maximilianstrasse 11, is open weekdays 10–1 and 2–6, Saturday 10–1, and one hour before the performance.

Theater an der Leopoldstrasse (⊠ Leopoldstr. 17, ☎ 089/343–803). It features the American Drama Group Europe, which gives English-language performances. No box office.

Munich also has several theaters for children. With pantomime such a strong part of the repertoire, the language problem disappears. The best of them are the **Münchner Theater für Kinder** (⊠ Dachauerstr. 46, ☎ 089/595–454 or 089/593–858)and the **Schauburg Theater der Jugend** (⊠

Franz-Joseph-Strasse 47, ☎ 089/237–21365). Three puppet theaters offer regular performances for children: the **Münchner Marionettentheater** (⊠ Blumenstr. 29a, ☎ 089/265–712), the **Marionettenbühne Zaubergarten** (⊠ Nikolaistr. 17, ☎ 089/271–3373), and **Otto Bille's Marionettenbühne** (⊠ Breiterangerstr. 15, ☎ 089/150–2168 or 089/310–1278). Munich is the winter quarters of the **Circus Krone** (⊠ Marsstr. 43, ☎ 089/558–166), which has its own permanent building. The circus performs there from Christmas until the end of March.

NIGHTLIFE

Munich's nighttime attractions vary with the seasons. The year starts with the abandon of *Fasching,* the Bavarian carnival time, which begins quietly in mid-November with the crowning of the King and Queen of Fools, expands with fancy-dress balls, and ends with a great street party on *Fasching Dienstag* (Shrove Tuesday). No sooner has Lent brought the sackcloth curtain down on Fasching than the local weather office is asked to predict when the spring sunshine will be warm enough to allow the city's 100 beer gardens to open. From then until late fall the beer garden dictates the style and pace of Munich's nightlife. When it rains, the indoor beer halls and taverns absorb the thirsty like blotting paper.

The beer gardens and most beer halls close at midnight, but there's no need to go home to bed then: Some bars and nightclubs are open until 6 AM. A word of caution about some of those bars: Most are run honestly, and prices are only slightly higher than normal, but a few may be unscrupulous. The seedier ones are near the main train station. Stick to beer or wine if you can, and pay as you go. And if you feel you're being duped, call the cops—the customer is usually, if not always, right.

Bars

Every Munich bar is singles territory. Try **Schumann's** (⊠ Maximilianstr. 36, ☎ 089/229–268) anytime after the curtain comes down at the nearby opera house (and watch the barmen shake those cocktails; closed Sat.). Wait till after midnight before venturing into the **Alter Simpl** (✉ Türkenstr. 57, ☎ 089/272–3083) for a sparkling crowd despite the gloomy surroundings. Back on fashionable Maximilianstrasse, **O'Reilly's Irish Cellar Pub** (✉ Maximilianstr. 29, ☎ 089/292–311) offers escape from the German bar scene, and it serves genuine Irish Guinness. Great Caribbean cocktails and a powerful Irish-German Black and Tan (Guinness and strong German beer) are served at the English nautical-style **Pusser's** bar (✉ Falkenturmstr. 9, ☎ 089/220–500); it replaced Munich's own Harry's Bar. Stiff competition is nearby at **Havana** (✉ Herrnstr. 3, ☎ 089/291–884), which does its darnedest to look like a rundown Cuban dive, although the chic clientele spoils those pretensions. Making contact at the **Wunderbar** (✉ Hochbrückenstr. 3, ☎ 089/295–118) is easier on Tuesday nights, when telephones are installed on the tables and at the bar and the place hums like a stygian switchboard. The lively (at any time) basement bar is run by an innovative young New Yorker.

Munich's gay scene is found between Sendlingertorplatz and Isartorplatz. Its most popular bars are **Nil** (✉ Hans-Sachs-Str. 2, ☎ 089/265–545), **Ochsengarten** (✉ Müllerstr. 47, ☎ 089/266–446), and **Old Mrs. Henderson** (✉ Müllerstr. 56, ☎ 089/267–176 or 089/263–469), which offers the city's best transvestite cabaret.

Clubs

Munich's club scene has fallen victim to changing tastes. Gone are the '60s-generation nightclubs combining a good restaurant, a dance combo, and high-class exotic dancers. In their place are tiny cabaret stages and even smaller strip bars. The cabarets, mostly in Schwabing, usually perform political satire in dialects that are incomprehensible to non-Germans.

The Bayerischer Hof's **Night Club** (✉ Promenadenpl. 2–6, ☎ 089/21200) has dancing to live music and a very lively bar. American visitors will also do well at the **Vier Jahreszeiten Kempinski** (✉ Maximilianstr. 17, ☎ 089/21250), where there's piano music until 9 and then dancing.

Discos

Schwabing is discoland, although it's getting ever greater competition from Munich's other "in" area, Haidhausen. A former Haidhausen factory has been converted into the city's largest rave scene: the **Kunstpark Ost** (⊠ Grafinger-str. 6, ☎ 089/490–42113). It has no less than 17 "enter-tainment areas," including discos, bars, and a huge slot-machine and computer-game hall. The Kunstpark Ost is a five-minute walk from the Ostbahnhof. Schwabing can still claim more than a dozen discos and music bars in the immediate area around its central square, the München-ner-Freiheit. One, the **Skyline** (☎ 089/333–131), is at the top of the Hertie department store that towers above the busy square. Other old-time favorites in a constantly chang-ing scene include **Peaches** (☎ 089/348–470), on nearby Feil-itzstrasse, and **Albatros** (☎ 089/344–972), just up the street on Occamstrasse (which is lined with lively clubs and pubs). Schwabing's central boulevard, Leopoldstrasse, also has its share of discos; **Singles** (⊠ Leopoldstr. 23, ☎ 089/ 343–535) is one of the trendiest. South of Schwabing **P1** (⊠ Prinzregentenstr., on west side of the Haus der Kunst, ☎ 089/294–252), **Maximilian's Nightclub** (⊠ Maximilianpl. 16, ☎ 089/223–252), and the **Park-Café** (⊠ Sophienstr. 7, ☎ 089/598–313) are the most fashionable discos in town, but you'll have to talk yourself past the doorman to join the chic crowds inside. The real ravers ride the S-bahn to Munich's Franz Josef Strauss Airport, alight at the Besucherpark station, and bop till dawn at the **Night Flight** (☎ 089/9759–7999), where it's becoming fashionable for package-tour travelers to start their holidays with a pre-check-in, early morning turn around the dance floor and a bar breakfast. **Nachtwerk** (⊠ Landsbergerstr. 185, ☎ 089/ 570–7390), in a converted factory, blasts out a range of sounds from punk to avant-garde nightly between 8 PM and 4 AM. Live bands also perform there regularly.

Jazz

Munich likes to think it's Germany's jazz capital, and to reinforce the claim, some beer gardens have taken to re-placing their brass bands with funky combos. Purists don't like it, but jazz enthusiasts are happy. The combination certainly works at **Waldwirtschaft Grosshesselohe** (✉ Georg-Kalb-Str. 3, ☎ 089/795–088), in the southern suburb of Grosshesselohe. Sundays are set aside for jazz, and if it's a nice day, the excursion is much recommended. Some city pubs and brewery taverns also set aside Sunday midday for jazz. The best of the jazz clubs are **Lamm's** (✉ Sendlinger-Tor-Platz 11, ☎ 089/591–963), **Nachtcafé** (✉ Maximilianpl. 5, ☎ 089/595–900), **Schwabinger Podium** (✉ Wagnerstr. 1, ☎ 089/399–482), and **Unterfahrt** (✉ Kirchenstr. 96, ☎ 089/448–279). The **CD** (✉ Ungererstr. 75) has a good jazz program featuring regular performances by vivacious English actress and singer Jenny Evans, who has a terrific voice and a warm welcome for visitors from the United States and Britain.

6 Outdoor Activities and Sports

THE **OLYMPIAPARK**, built for the 1972 Olympics, is one of the largest sports and recreation centers in Europe. For **general information** about clubs, organizations, and events, contact the **Haus des Sport** (⌧ Neuhauserstr. 26, ☎ 089/233–6224).

Beaches and Water Sports

There is sailing and windsurfing on Ammersee and Starnbergersee. Windsurfers should pay attention to restricted areas at bathing beaches. Information on sailing is available from **Bayrischer Segler-Verband** (⌧ Georg-Brauchle-Ring 93, ☎ 089/157–02366). Information on windsurfing is available from **Verband der Deutschen Windsurfing Schulen** (⌧ Weilheim, ☎ 0881/5267).

Golf

Munich Golf Club has two courses that admit visitors on weekdays. Visitors must be members of a club at home. Its 18-hole course is at Strasslach in the suburb of Grünwald, south of the city (☎ 08170/450). Its nine-hole course is more centrally located, at Thalkirchen, on the Isar River (☎ 089/723–1304). The greens fee is DM 75 for both courses.

Ice-Skating

There is an indoor ice rink at the **Eissportstadion** in Olympiapark (⌧ Spiridon-Louis-Ring 3)and outdoor rinks at **Prinzregenten Stadium** (⌧ Prinzregentenstr. 80) and **Eisbahn-West** (⌧ Agnes-Bernauer Str. 241). There is outdoor skating in winter on the lake in the **Englischer Garten** and on the **Nymphenburger Canal,** where you can also go curling (*Eisstockschiessen*) by renting equipment from little wooden huts, which also sell hot drinks. Players rent sections of machine-smoothed ice on the canal. Watch out for the *Gefahr* (danger) signs warning of thin ice. Additional information is available from **Bayerischer Eissportverband** (⌧ Georg-Brauchle-Ring 93, ☎ 089/157–9920).

Jogging

The best place to jog is the **Englischer Garten** (U-bahn: Münchner-Freiheit or Universität), which is 11 km (7 mi) around and has lakes and dirt and asphalt paths. You can also jog through **Olympiapark** (U-bahn: Olympiazentrum). A pleasant morning or evening jog can be had along the **Isar River.** The 500-acre park of **Schloss Nymphenburg** is

ideal for running. For a longer jog along the Isar River, take
the S-bahn to Unterföhring and pace yourself back to
Münchner-Freiheit—a distance of 6½ km (4 mi).

Rowing

Rowboats can be rented on the southern bank of the
Olympiasee in Olympiapark and at the **Kleinhesseloher See**
in the Englischer Garten.

Swimming

You can try swimming outdoors in the Isar River at Maria-
Einsiedel, but be warned that because the river flows from
the Alps the water is frigid even in summer. Warmer swimming can be found off the beaches of the lakes near Munich—for example, the **Ammersee** and **Starnbergersee.**
There are pools at **Cosima Bad** (⊠ Englschalkingerstr. and
Cosimastr., Bogenhausen), with man-made waves; **Dante-
bad** (⊠ Dantestr. 6); **Nordbad** (⊠ Schleissheimerstr. 142,
in the Schwabing District); **Michaelibad** (⊠ Heinrich-
Wieland-Str. 24); **Olympia-Schwimmhalle** (⊠ Olympiapark); and **Müllersches Volksbad** (⊠ Rosenheimerstr. 1).

Tennis

There are indoor and outdoor courts at **Münchnerstrasse
15,** in München-Unterföhring; at the corner of **Drygalski-
Allee** and **Kistlerhofstrasse,** in München-Fürstenried; and
at **Rothof Sportanlage** (⊠ Denningerstr., behind the Ara-
bella and Sheraton hotels). In addition, there are about 200
outdoor courts all over Munich. Many can be booked via
Sport Scheck (☎ 089/21660), which has installations around
town. Prices vary from DM 18 to DM 25 an hour, depending
on the time of day. Full details on tennis in Munich are available from the **Bayerischer Tennis Verband** (⊠ Georg-
Brauchle-Ring 93, ☎ 089/157–02640).

7 Shopping

MUNICH HAS an immense central shopping area, 2 km (1 mi) of pedestrian streets stretching from the train station to Marienplatz and north to Odeonsplatz. The two main streets here are Neuhauserstrasse and Kaufingerstrasse, the sites of most major department stores. For upscale shopping, Maximilianstrasse, Residenzstrasse, and Theatinerstrasse are unbeatable and contain a fine array of classy and tempting stores that are the equal of any in Europe. Schwabing, north of the university, has several of the city's most intriguing and offbeat shopping streets—Schellingstrasse and Hohenzollernstrasse are two to try.

Antiques

Bavarian antiques can be found in the many small shops around the Viktualienmarkt; Westenriederstrasse is lined with antiques shops. Also try the area north of the university; Türkenstrasse, Theresienstrasse, and Barerstrasse are all filled with stores that sell antiques. **Seidl Antiquitäten** (⊠ Sieges-Str. 21, near Münchner Freiheit, ☎ 089/349–568) is so full of antique goods you might literally stumble over what you've always wanted to put on that corner of the mantelpiece. **Carl Jagemann's** (⊠ Residenzstr. 3, ☎ 089/225–493) has been in the antiques business for more than a century, despite the shop's high prices. Perhaps friendly and knowledgeable service is the secret of its success. **Robert Müller's** antiques shop (⊠ Westenriederstr. 4, ☎ 089/221–726) is where you'll find German military memorabilia (spiked helmets from the First World War sell for upwards of DM 600). Strictly for window shopping—unless you're looking for something really rare and special, and money's no object—are the exclusive shops lining Prannerstrasse, at the rear of the Hotel Bayerischer Hof.

Horst Fuchs (⊠ Westenriederstr. 17, ☎ 089/223–791) has one of Munich's best selections of antique beer mugs. His crowded shelves also hide sentimental embroidered pictures, kitschy souvenirs, and other amusing and inexpensive German knickknacks.

In **Antike Uhren Eder** (⊠ Prannerstr. 4, in the Hotel Bayerischer Hof building, ☎ 089/220–305), the silence is broken only by the ticking of dozens of highly valuable German antique clocks and by discreet bargaining over the high prices. The nearby **Antike Uhren H. Schley** (⊠ Kardinal-Faulhaber-Str. 14a, ☎ 089/226–188) also specializes in antique clocks.

Interesting and/or cheap antiques and assorted junk from all over eastern Europe are laid out at the weekend **flea markets** beneath the Donnersberger railway bridge on Arnfulstrasse.

Department Stores

Hertie (⊠ Bahnhofpl. 7, ☎ 089/55120), occupying an entire city block between the train station and Karlsplatz, is the largest and, some claim, the best department store in the city. The basement has a high-class delicatessen with champagne bar and a stand-up bistro offering a daily changing menu that puts many high-price Munich restaurants to shame. Hertie's Schwabing branch (⊠ at the square known as Münchner-Freiheit) was recently given a top-to-bottom face-lift, which left it loaded with high-gloss steel and glass. **Kaufhof** has two central Munich stores (⊠ Karlspl. 2, opposite Hertie, ☎ 089/51250; ⊠ Karlspl. and Marienpl., ☎ 089/231–851). Both offer a range of mid-price goods. If you catch an end-of-season sale, you're sure to get a bargain.

Karstadt (⊠ Neuhauserstr. 18, ☎ 089/290–230), in the 100-year-old Haus Oberpollinger, at the start of the Kaufingerstrasse shopping mall, is another high-class department store, with a very wide range of Bavarian arts and crafts. **Ludwig Beck** (⊠ Marienpl. 11, ☎ 089/236–910) is one of the smaller department stores, but it's packed from top to bottom with highly original wares—from fine feather boas to roughly finished Bavarian pottery. It comes into its own as Christmas approaches, when a series of booths, each delicately and lovingly decorated, is occupied by craftspeople turning out traditional German toys and decorations. **Hirmer** (⊠ Kaufingerstr. 28, ☎ 089/236–830) has Munich's most comprehensive collection of German-made men's clothes, with a markedly friendly and knowledgeable staff. **K & L Ruppert** (⊠ Kaufingerstr. 15, ☎ 089/231–1470) has a good, fashionable range of German-made clothes in the lower price brackets.

76

Antike Uhren
Eder, **30**
Antike Uhren H.
Schley, **29**
Arcade, **11**
Barerstrasse, **33**
Bayerischer
Kunstgewer-
beverein, **6**
Carl
Jagemann's, **25**
Dallmayr, **23**
Geschenk Alm, **18**
Hertie, **1, 39**
Hirmer, **10**
Hohenzollern-
strasse, **37**
Horst Fuchs, **20**
K & L Ruppert, **9**
Karstadt, **5**
Kaufhof, **2, 12**
Kaufingerstrasse, **7**
Kaufinger Tor, **8**
Kunstring
Meissen, **35**
Lederhosen
Wagner, **17**
Loden-Frey, **26**
Ludwig Beck, **16**
Ludwig Mory, **15**
Maximilian-
strasse, **40**
Neuhauser-
strasse, **4**
Nymphenburg
store, **34**
Obletter's, **3, 14**
Otto Kellnberger's
Holzhandlung, **18**
Residenzstrasse, **27**
Robert Müller's, **21**
Schellingstrasse, **36**
Sebastian
Wesely, **13**
Seidl
Antiquitäten, **38**
Theatinerstrasse, **28**
Theresienstrasse, **32**
Türkenstrasse, **31**
Viktualienmarkt, **19**
Wallach, **24**
Zerwick
Gewölbe, **22**

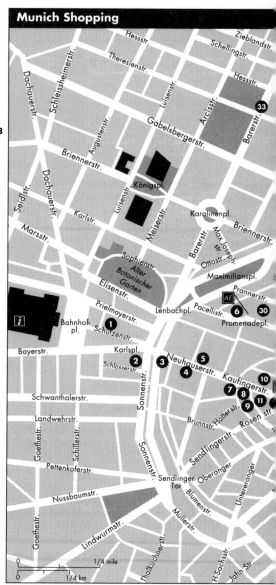

Munich Shopping

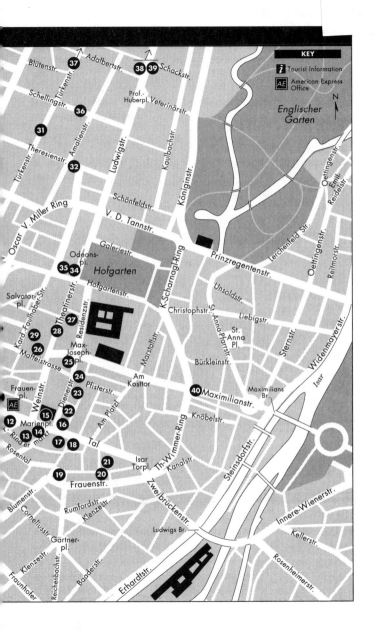

Folk Costumes

Those who feel the need to deck themselves out in lederhosen or a dirndl, or to sport a green loden coat and a little pointed hat with feathers, have a wide choice in the
Bavarian capital. Among the shops to visit are **Loden-Frey**
(✉ Maffeistr. 7–9, ☎ 089/210–390), **Wallach** (✉ Residenzstr. 3, ☎ 089/220–871), and **Lederhosen Wagner** (✉
Tal 77, ☎ 089/225–697).

Food Markets

Munich's **Viktualienmarkt** is *the* place to shop. Just south
of Marienplatz, it's home to an array of colorful stands that
sell everything from cheese to sausages, from flowers to wine.
A visit here is more than just an excuse to buy picnic mak-
ings; it's central to an understanding of the easy-come-
easy-go nature of Müncheners. If you are staying in the
Schwabing area, the daily market at **Elisabethplatz** is worth
a visit—it's much, much smaller than the Viktualienmarkt,
but the range and quality of produce are comparable.

Dallmayr (✉ Dienerstr. 14–15, ☎ 089/21350) is an elegant gourmet food store, with delights ranging from the most
exotic fruits to English jams, served by efficient Munich ma-
trons in smart blue-and-white linen costumes. The store's
famous specialty is coffee, with more than 50 varieties to
blend as you wish. There's also an enormous range of
breads and a temperature-controlled cigar room.

The **Zerwick Gewölbe** (✉ Ledererstr. 3, ☎ 089/226–824)
is Munich's oldest venison shop, with a mouthwatering se-
lection of smoked meats, including wild boar.

Gifts

Munich is a city of beer, and items related to its consumption are obvious choices for souvenirs and gifts. Visit **Ludwig Mory** (✉ Marienpl. 8, ☎ 089/224–542) or **Sebastian
Wesely** (✉ Peterspl., ☎ 089/264–519).

Munich is the home of the famous **Nymphenburg Porcelain** factory. The Nymphenburg store (✉ corner of Odeonspl. and Briennerstr., ☎ 089/282–428) resembles a drawing
room of the famous Munich palace, with dove-gray soft
furnishings and the delicate, expensive porcelain safely
locked away in bowfront cabinets. You can also buy direct

from the factory, on the grounds of Schloss Nymphenburg (⊠ Nördliches Schlossrondell 8, ☎ 089/1291888). For Dresden and Meissen ware, go to **Kunstring Meissen** (⊠ Briennerstr. 4, ☎ 089/281–532).

Bavarian craftsmen and craftswomen have a showplace of their own, the **Bayerischer Kunstgewerbeverein**(⊠ Pacellistr. 10, ☎ 089/29162928); here you'll find every kind of handicraft and delicate workmanship, from glass and pottery to textiles, all made in Bavaria.

Otto Kellnberger's Holzhandlung (⊠ Heiliggeiststr. 7–8, ☎ 089/226–479) specializes in another Bavarian craft—woodwork. **Geschenk Alm** (⊠ Heiliggeiststr. 7–8, ☎ 089/225–147) has nooks and crannies where brushes of every kind are stowed. Looking for that pig's-bristle brush to get to the bottom of tall champagne glasses? This is the place to find it.

Obletter's (⊠ Karlspl. 11–12, ☎ 089/231–8601; ⊠ Neuhauserstr. 31, ☎ 089/231–8601; ⊠ Marienpl., ☎ 089/264–062) has a total of five floors packed with toys, many of them handmade German playthings of great charm and quality.

Malls

Two new shopping malls have opened in recent years in the main pedestrian area, near Kaufingerstrasse and Neuhauserstrasse. **Kaufinger Tor** (⊠ Kaufingerstr. 117) has several floors of boutiques and cafés packed neatly together under a high glass roof. The aptly named **Arcade** (⊠ Neuhauserstr. 5) is where the young Munich crowd finds the best designer jeans and chunky jewelry.

8 Side Trips from Munich

MUNICH'S excellent suburban railway network, the S-bahn, brings several outlying towns and attractive rural areas within easy reach for a day's excursion. The two nearest lakes, Ammersee and Starnbergersee, are highly recommended in summer and winter alike, particularly for visitors who want to escape the bustle of Munich for a day. Dachau attracts overseas visitors, mostly because of its concentration-camp memorial site, but it's an attractive and historic town in its own right. Landshut, north of Munich, is way off the tourist track, but if it were the same distance south of Munich, this jewel of a Bavarian market town would have difficulty accommodating the crush. Wasserburg am Inn is another charming Bavarian town, held in the narrow embrace of the Inn River, and it's easily incorporated into an excursion to the nearby Chiemsee Lake. All these destinations have a wide choice of dining possibilities and hotels.

Ammersee

The Ammersee is the country cousin of the better-known, more cosmopolitan Starnbergersee, and many Bavarians (and tourists, too) like it all the more as a result. Fashionable Munich cosmopolites of centuries past thought it too distant for an excursion, not to mention too rustic for their sophisticated tastes. So the shores remained relatively free of the villas and parks that ring the Starnbergersee, and even though the upscale holiday homes of Munich's moneyed classes today claim some stretches of the eastern shore, the Ammersee still offers more open areas for bathing and boating than the bigger lake to the west. Bicyclists can circle the 19-km-long (12-mi-long) lake (it's nearly 6 km, or 4 mi, across at its widest point) on a path that rarely loses sight of the water. Hikers can spread out the tour for two or three days, staying overnight in any of the comfortable inns along the way. Dinghy sailors and windsurfers can zip across in minutes with the help of the Alpine winds that swoop down from the mountains. A ferry boat cruises the lake at regular intervals during summer, dropping and picking up passengers at several pier stops. Join it at Herrsching.

Around Munich

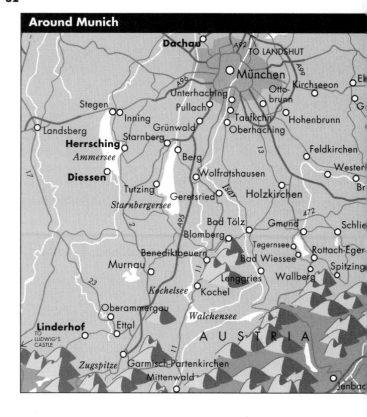

TO LANDSHUT

Dachau

München

Ottobrunn

Kirchseeon

El

Unterhaching

Pullach

Taufkchn

Hohenbrunn

G

Stegen

Inning

Oberhaching

Landsberg

Grünwald

Feldkirchen

Starnberg

Herrsching

Wester

Ammersee

Berg

Br

Diessen

Wolfratshausen

Holzkirchen

Tutzing

Geretsried

Starnbergersee

Bad Tölz

Gmund

Schlie

Blomberg

Tegernsee

Rottach-Eger

Benediktbeuern

Bad Wiessee

Murnau

Spitzing

Lenggries

Wallberg

Kochelsee

Kochel

Oberammergau

Walchensee

Linderhof

Ettal

TO
LUDWIG'S
CASTLE

AUSTRIA

Zugspitze

Garmisch-Partenkirchen

Mittenwald

Jenbac

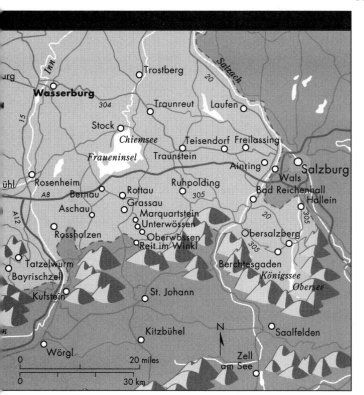

Exploring Ammersee

Herrsching has a delightful promenade, part of which winds through the resort's park. The 100-year-old villa that sits so comfortably in the park, overlooking the lake and the Alps beyond, seems as if it were built by Ludwig II, such is the romantic and fanciful mixture of medieval turrets and Renaissance-style facades. It was actually built for the artist Ludwig Scheuermann in the late 19th century and became a favorite meeting place for Munich and Bavarian artists. It is now a municipal cultural center and the scene of chamber-music concerts on some summer weekends.

The Benedictine monastery of **Andechs,** one of southern Bavaria's most famous places of pilgrimage, lies 5 km (3 mi) south of Herrsching. You can reach it on Bus 951 (connecting Ammersee and Starnbergersee). The crowds of pilgrims are drawn not only by the beauty of the hilltop monastery—its 15th-century pilgrimage church decked out with glorious rococo decoration in the mid-18th century and a repository of religious relics said to have been brought from the Holy Land 1,000 years ago—but also by the beer brewed there. The monastery makes its own cheese as well, and it's an excellent accompaniment to the rich, almost black, beer. You can enjoy both at large wood tables in the monastery tavern or on the terrace outside. The son of the last Austro-Hungarian emperor, Archduke Otto von Hapsburg, lives beside the lake. He celebrated his 80th birthday in the church in 1992, with a family party following in the tavern. ☼ *Daily 7–7.*

The little town of **Diessen,** with its magnificent Baroque abbey-church, is situated at the southwest corner of the lake. Step inside the abbey to admire its opulent stucco decoration and sumptuous gilt-and-marble altar. Visit the church in late afternoon, when the light falls sharply on its crisp gray, white, and gold facade, etching the pencil-like tower and spire against the darkening sky over the lake. Don't go without at least peeping into neighboring St. Stephen's courtyard, its cloisters smothered in wild roses.

Dining

ANDECHS

The **Hotel Zur Post** (⊠ Starnberger Str. 2, ☎ 08152/3433; $), at the foot of the Andechs monastery hill, rears its own deer, and venison finds its way onto the menu every day from October through April.

The **Hotel-Gasthof-Seefelder Hof** (⊠ Alexander-Koester-Weg 6, ☎ 08807/1022; $) has a cozy restaurant serving Bavarian specialties and a delightful beer garden.

The **Hotel Promenade** (⊠ Summerstr. 6, ☎ 08152/1350; $) is one of the best of the several idyllic terrace restaurants you'll find along the lakeside promenade. Rivaling it is the **Artis** restaurant in the stately, newly renovated **Ammersee-Hotel** (⊠ Summerstr. 32, ☎ 08152/2011; $). The **Piushof** (⊠ Schönbichlstr. 18, ☎ 08152/1007; $) lacks a lake view, but its beamed and pillared restaurant has an excellent menu of seasonal Bavarian specialties.

Ammersee A to Z

By Car. Take Autobahn 96—follow the signs to Lindau—and 20 km (12 mi) west of Munich take the exit for Herrsching, the lake's principal town. Herrsching is 40 km (25 mi) from Munich.

By Train. Herrsching, on the east bank of the lake, is the end of the S-bahn 5 suburban line, a half-hour ride from Munich's central Marienplatz. From Herrsching station, Bus 952 runs north along the lake, and Bus 951 runs south.

Verkehrsamt (⊠ Bahnhofspl. 2, ☎ 08152/5227).

Dachau

The first Nazi concentration camp was built just outside this town. Dachau preserves the memory of the camp and the horrors perpetrated there with deep contrition while trying, with commendable discretion, to signal that it also has other things to offer visitors. It's older than nearby Munich, for example, with local records going back to the time of Charlemagne in the 9th century. And it's a handsome town, too, built on a hilltop with fine views of Munich and the Alps.

Exploring Dachau

The site of the infamous camp, now the **KZ-Gedenkstätte Dachau** (Dachau Concentration Camp Memorial), is just outside the town. Photographs, contemporary documents, the few remaining cell blocks, and the grim crematorium create a somber and moving picture of the camp, where many tens of thousands lost their lives. To reach the memorial by car, leave the center of the town along Schleissheimerstrasse and turn left into Alte Römerstrasse; the site is on the left. By public transport, take Bus 722 from the Dachau S-bahn train station to Robert-Boschstrasse and walk along Alte Römerstrasse for 100 yards, or board Bus 720 and get off at Ratiborer Strasse. ⊠ *Alte Römerstr. 75,* ☎ *08121/ 1741.* 🎫 *Free.* ☉ *Tues.–Sun. 9–5. Guided English tour weekends at 12:30, English documentary film daily at 11:30 and 3:30.*

Schloss Dachau, the hilltop castle, dominates the town. What you'll see is the one remaining wing of a palace built by the Munich architect Josef Effner for the Wittelsbach ruler Max Emanuel in 1715, a replacement for the original castle built during the 15th century. During the Napoleonic Wars at the beginning of the 19th century the palace served as a field hospital, treating French and Russian casualties from the Battle of Austerlitz (1805). The wars made a casualty, too, of the palace, and three of the four wings were demolished by order of King Max Joseph I. What's left is a handsome cream-and-white building, with an elegant pillared and lantern-hung café on the ground floor and the former ballroom above. Concerts are regularly held here, beneath a richly decorated and carved ceiling, with painted panels representing characters from ancient mythology. The east-facing terrace affords panoramic views of Munich and, on fine days, the distant Alps, while in summer the café opens out onto a very attractive south-facing terrace overlooking pretty, orchardlike gardens. There's also a 250-year-old *Schlossbrauerei* (castle brewery), which hosts the town's own beer and music festival each year during the first half of August. ⊠ *Schlosspl.,* ☎ *08131/87923.* 🎫 *DM 2, tour DM 5.* ☉ *May–Sept., weekends 2–5; tour of town and Schloss May–mid-Oct., Sat. 10:30.*

BONUS MILES MAKE
GREAT SOUVENIRS.

Earn Miles With
Your MCI Card.

Take the MCI Card along on
this trip and start earning
miles for the next one. You'll
earn frequent flyer miles on all
your calls and save with the low
rates you've come to expect
from MCI. Before you know it,
you'll be on your way to some
other international destination.

Sign up for MCI by calling
1-800-FLY-FREE

Earn Frequent Flyer Miles.

 AmericanAirlines®
AAdvantage®

 Continental Airlines
OnePass

 ▲ Delta Air Lines
SkyMiles®

 NORTHWEST
AIRLINES
WORLDPERKS®

✈ MILEAGE PLUS.
United Airlines

US AIRWAYS
DIVIDEND MILES

Is this a great time, or what? :-)

 MCI

Easy To Call Home.

1. To use your MCI Card, just dial the
   WorldPhone access number of the country
   you're calling from.
2. Dial or give the operator your MCI Card
   number.
3. Dial or give the number you're calling.

# Austria (CC) ♦	022-903-012
# Belarus (CC)	
From Brest, Vitebsk, Grodno, Minsk	8-800-103
From Gomel and Mogilev regions	8-10-800-103
# Belgium (CC) ♦	0800-10012
# Bulgaria	00800-0001
# Croatia (CC) ★	0800-22-0112
# Czech Republic (CC) ♦	00-42-000112
# Denmark (CC) ♦	8001-0022
# Finland (CC) ♦	08001-102-80
# France (CC) ♦	0-800-99-0019
# Germany (CC)	0800-888-8000
# Greece (CC) ♦	00-800-1211
# Hungary (CC) ♦	00▼800-01411
# Iceland (CC) ♦	800-9002
# Ireland (CC)	1-800-55-1001
# Italy (CC) ♦	172-1022
# Kazakhstan (CC)	8-800-131-4321
# Liechtenstein (CC) ♦	0800-89-0222
# Luxembourg	0800-0112
# Monaco (CC) ♦	800-90-019
# Netherlands (CC) ♦	0800-022-9122
# Norway (CC) ♦	800-19912
# Poland (CC) ÷	00-800-111-21-22
# Portugal (CC) ÷	05-017-1234
Romania (CC) ÷	01-800-1800
# Russia (CC) ÷ ♦	
To call using ROSTELCOM ■	747-3322
For a Russian-speaking operator	747-3320
To call using SOVINTEL ■	960-2222
# San Marino (CC) ♦	172-1022
# Slovak Republic (CC)	00-421-00112
# Slovenia	080-8808
# Spain (CC)	900-99-0014
# Sweden (CC) ♦	020-795-922
# Switzerland (CC) ♦	0800-89-0222
# Turkey (CC) ♦	00-8001-1177
# Ukraine (CC) ÷	8▼10-013
# United Kingdom (CC)	
To call using BT ■	0800-89-0222
To call using C&W ■	0500-89-0222
# Vatican City (CC)	172-1022

#Automation available from most locations. (CC) Country-to-
country calling available to/from most international locations.
♦ Public phones may require deposit of coin or phone card for
dial tone. ★ Not available from public pay phones. ▼ Wait for
second dial tone. ÷ Limited availability. ■ International communi-
cations carrier. Limit one bonus program per MCI account. Terms
and conditions apply. All airline program rules and conditions
apply. © 1998 MCI Telecommunications Corporation. All rights
reserved. Is this a great time, or what? is a service mark of MCI.

CHASE

Flying to France on Friday? Get Francs from Chase on Thursday. Call Currency To Go at 935-9935 for overnight delivery.

CHASE CURRENCY TO GO 935-9935

$\mathcal{O}$r pounds for London. Or Deutschmarks for Düsseldorf. Or any of 75 foreign currencies. Call **Chase Currency To Go**^{SM} at **935-9935** in area codes 212, 718, 914, 516 and Rochester, N.Y.; all other area codes call 1-800-935-9935. We'll deliver directly to your door.* Overnight. And there are no exchange fees. Let Chase make your trip an easier one.

CHASE. The right relationship is everything.^{SM}

St. Jacob, Dachau's parish church, was built in the early 16th century in late-Renaissance style on the foundations of a 14th-century Gothic building. Baroque features and a characteristic onion dome were added in the late 17th century. On the south wall you can admire a very fine 17th-century sundial clock. A visit to the church is included in the guided tour of the town (May–mid-October, Saturday 10:30). ⊠ *Konrad-Adenauer-Str. 7,* ⊙ *Daily 7–7.*

Dachau served as a lively **artists' colony** during the 19th century, and the tradition lives on. The picturesque houses designed for the colony line Hermann-Stockmann-Strasse and part of Münchner Strasse, and many of them are still the homes of successful artists. The **Gemäldegalerie** displays the works of many of the town's 19th-century artists. ⊠ *Konrad-Adenauer-Str. 3,* ☎ *08131/567–516.* ⌧ *DM 3.* ⊙ *Wed.–Fri. 11–5, weekends 1–5.*

Dining and Lodging

The **Bräustüberl** (⊠ Schlossstr. 8, ☎ 08131/72553; $), 100 yards from the castle, has a shady beer garden for summer lunches and a cozy tavern for year-round Bavarian-style eating and drinking. The solid, historic **Zieglerbräu** (⊠ Konrad-Adenauer-Str. 8, ☎ 08131/4074; $–$$), once a 17th-century brewer's home, is now a wood-paneled restaurant; it's next to the ivy-covered Town Hall. The **Hörhammerbräu** (⊠ Konrad-Adenauer-Str. 12, ☎ 08131/4711; $–$$) serves its own beer, as well as hearty Bavarian dishes costing less than DM 20. The Hörhammerbräu also has 21 reasonably priced guest rooms.

Dachau A to Z

ARRIVING AND DEPARTING

By Car. Dachau is 20 km (12 mi) northwest of Munich. Take the B–12 country road, or the Stuttgart Autobahn to the Dachau exit.

By Train. Dachau is on the S-bahn No. 2 suburban line, a 20-minute ride from Munich's Marienplatz.

VISITOR INFORMATION

Verkehrsverein Dachau (⊠ Konrad-Adenauer-Str. 3, ☎ 08131/84566).

Landshut

If fortune had placed Landshut 64 km (40 mi) south of Munich, in the protective folds of the Alpine foothills, instead of the same distance north, in the dull flatlands of Lower Bavaria, this delightful, historic town would have been overrun by visitors long ago. All the same, Landshut's geographical misfortune is the discerning visitor's good luck, for the town is never overcrowded, with the possible exception of the three summer weeks every four years when the *Landshuter Hochzeit* (Landshut Wedding) is celebrated. The next celebration is in 2001, and then a visit to Landshut is really a must on any tour of this part of Germany. The festival commemorates the marriage in 1475 of Prince George of Bayern-Landshut, son of the expressively named Ludwig the Rich, to Princess Hedwig, daughter of the king of Poland. The entire town is swept away in a colorful reconstruction of the event, which increases its already regal importance and helps give it the majestic air you'll still find within its ancient walls.

Exploring Landshut

Landshut has two magnificent cobblestone market streets. The one in **Altstadt** (Old Town) is considered by many to be the most beautiful city street in Germany; the one in **Neustadt** (New Town) projects its own special appeal. The two streets run parallel to each other, tracing a course between the Isar River and the heights overlooking the town. A steep path from Altstadt takes you up to **Burg Trausnitz,** sitting commandingly on the heights. This castle was begun in 1204 and accommodated the Wittelsbach dukes of Bayern-Landshut until 1503. ☎ *0871/22638. ⌦ DM 4, including guided tour. ☉ Apr.–Sept., daily 9–noon and 1–5; Oct.–Mar., daily 10–noon and 1–4.*

The **Stadtresidenz** in Altstadt was the first Italian Renaissance building of its kind north of the Alps. During the 16th century the Wittelsbachs moved to Altstadt and into this palace. The Renaissance facade of the palace forms an almost modest part of the architectural splendor and integrity of Altstadt, where even the ubiquitous McDonald's has to serve its hamburgers behind a baroque exterior. ☎ *0871/22638. ⌦ DM 3. ☉ Apr.–Sept., daily 9–noon and 1–5; Oct.–Mar., daily 10–noon and 1–4.*

St. Martin's Church, with the tallest brick church tower in the world, soars above the other buildings with its 436-ft tower and bristling spire. The church contains some magnificent Gothic treasures and a 16th-century carved Madonna. Moreover, it is surely the only church in the world to contain an image of Hitler, albeit in a devilish pose. The Führer and other Nazi leaders are portrayed as executioners in a 1946 stained-glass window showing the martyrdom of St. Kastulus. In the nave of the church is a clear and helpful description of its history and its treasures, an aid to English-speaking visitors that could profitably be copied by other churches and historical sites in Germany. ☎ 0871/24277. ☉ *Apr.–Sept., daily 7–6:30; Oct.–Mar., daily 7–5.*

German President Roman Herzog opened an important new cultural attraction in Landshut in 1998: the **Skulpturenmuseum im Hofberg,** a comprehensive collection of sculptures from Gothic times to contemporary works. The museum was built into the old city walls. ⊠ *Im HofbergIm Hofberg,* ☎ *0871/8902. Call ahead for hours and admission cost.*

Dining
There are several attractive **Bavarian-style restaurants** in Altstadt and Neustadt, most of them with charming beer gardens. The best are **Brauereigasthof Ainmiller** (⊠ Altstadt 195, ☎ 0871/21163; $), **Gasthaus Schwabl** (⊠ Neustadt 500, ☎ 0871/23930; $), **Zum Hofreiter** (⊠ Neustadt 505, ☎ 0871/24402; $), and the **Hotel Goldene Sonne** (⊠ Neustadt 520, ☎ 0871/92530; $).

The **Klausenberg Panorama-Restaurant** (⊠ Klausenberg 17; $) has a terrace with a fine view of the town and the surrounding countryside. If you're looking for an authentic Bavarian dining experience, make your way to the old Episcopal town of Freising, halfway between Landshut and Munich. Here you'll find the **Bayerische Staatsbrauerei Weihenstephan** (☎ 08161/13004; $), the world's oldest brewery (dating from AD 1040), where you can select from 11 different brews. Freising is the final stop on the S-1 suburban railway line from Munich and one stop from Landshut by express train.

Lodging

Landshut has several hotels and a handful of reasonably priced, comfortable inns. The **Lindner Hotel Kaiserhof** (✉ Papiererstr. 2, ☎ 0871/6870, FAX 0871/687–403; $$$) is housed in an attractive 18th-century-style riverside building. At the **Romantik Hotel Fürstenhof** (✉ Stethaimerstr. 3, ☎ 0871/92550, FAX 0871/925–544; $$$) you'll rest your head in a tastefully modernized villa. **Hotel Goldene Sonne** (✉ Neustadt 520, ☎ 0871/92530, FAX 0871/925–3350; $$$) is a historic inn in the Old Town.

In 1996 the **Hotel Schloss Schönbrunn** (✉ Schönbrunn 1, ☎ 0871/95220, FAX 0871/952–2222; $$$) opened in the Schloss Schönbrunn palace, on the edge of Landshut. Rooms are suitably palatial and overlook the superb palace grounds.

Landshut A to Z

ARRIVING AND DEPARTING

By Car. Landshut is a 45-minute drive northwest from Munich on either Autobahn A–92—follow the signs to Deggendorf—or the B–11 highway.

By Train. Landshut is on the Plattling–Regensburg–Passau line, a 40-minute ride by express train from Munich.

VISITOR INFORMATION

Verkehrsverein (✉ Altstadt 315, ☎ 0871/922–050).

Starnbergersee

The Starnbergersee was one of Europe's first pleasure grounds. Royal coaches trundled out from Munich to its wooded banks in the Baroque years of the 17th century; in 1663 Elector Ferdinand Maria threw a huge shipboard party at which 500 guests wined and dined as 100 oarsmen propelled them around the lake. Today pleasure steamers perform the same task for visitors of less-than-noble rank. The lake is still lined with the Baroque palaces of Bavaria's aristocracy, but their owners must now share the lakeside with public parks, beaches, and boatyards. The Starnbergersee is one of Bavaria's largest lakes—19 km (12 mi) long and 5 km (3 mi) across at its widest point—so there's plenty of room for swimmers, sailors, and Windsurfers. On its west shore is one of Germany's finest golf courses, but it's about as difficult for the casual visitor to play a game there as it was for a Munich commoner to win an invitation to one of Prince Ferdinand's boating parties. Those on the trail of Ludwig II should note that Starnbergersee (beside the village of Berg) was where the doomed monarch met his watery death under circumstances that remain a mystery.

Exploring Starnbergersee

At Berg you'll find the **King Ludwig II Memorial Chapel,** on the eastern shore of the lake. A well-marked path leads through thick woods to the chapel, built near the point in the lake where the king's body was found on June 13, 1886. He had been confined in nearby Berg Castle after the Bavarian government took action against his withdrawal from reality and into an expensive castle-building fantasyland. Look for the cross in the lake, which marks the point where his body was recovered.

The castle of **Possenhofen,** home of Ludwig's favorite cousin, Sisi, stands on the western shore of Starnbergersee, practically opposite Berg. Local lore says they used to send affectionate messages across the lake to each other. Sisi married the Austrian emperor Franz Joseph I but frequently returned to the Starnbergersee; she spent more than 20 consecutive summers in the lakeside castle, now a luxury hotel, the **Kaiserin Elisabeth.** ✉ *D-82340 Feldafing,* ☎ *08157/1013.*

Just offshore is the tiny **Roseninsel** (Rose Island), where King Maximilian II built a summer villa. You can swim to its tree-fringed shores or sail across in a dinghy or on a Windsurfer (Possenhofen's boatyard is one of the lake's many rental points).

Dining and Lodging

The fine old **Bayerischer Hof** (✉ Bahnhofstr. 12, D–80333, ☎ 08151/2750; $$) has an elegant café with a sunny terrace, a Bavarian tavern named Fisher Stübe, and reasonably priced guest rooms. If you feel like a splurge, book the beamed König-Ludwig suite, with a terrace commanding a breathtaking view of the lake and the mountains beyond. The **Gasthof Zur Sonne** (✉ Hanfelder Str. 7, ☎ 08151/2060; $$) has no lake views but lake fish land every day on the menu of its beamed and wood-paneled restaurant. The **Seer-estaurant Undosa** (⊠ Seepromenade 1, ☎ 08151/8021; $$), where the atmosphere is always boisterous, has uninterrupted lake views for your enjoyment. Farther down the lake, on the outskirts of Possenhofen, is the **Forsthaus am See** (⊠ Am See 1, Pocking-Possenhofen, ☎ 08157/93010; $$), where you dine beneath a carved panel ceiling imported from Austria's South Tyrol. The restaurant has a lakeside beer garden and its own pier for guests who arrive by boat. From Tutzing, at the end of the S-6 suburban line, a short walk up into the hills leads to the **Forsthaus Ilka-Höhe** (☎ 08158/8242; $$), a rustic lodge with a fine view of the lake and excellent Bavarian food. It's closed Monday and Tuesday and during the Christmas holidays. On the side of the lake near the Berg Castle grounds and the King Ludwig II Memorial Chapel, try the **Dorint Seehotel Leoni** (⊠ Assenbucherstr. 44, Berg-Leoni; $), where you can also rent bicycles (☎ 08151/5060). The **Hotel Schloss Berg** (⊠ Seestrasse 17, ☎ 08151/9630; $) has a lakeside dining terrace.

Starnbergersee A to Z

ARRIVING AND DEPARTING

By Car. The north end of the lake, where the resort of Starnberg sits in stately beauty, is a 30-minute drive from Munich on Autobahn A–95. Follow the signs to Garmisch and take the Starnberg exit. Country roads then skirt the west and east banks of the lake.

By Train. The S-bahn 6 suburban line runs from Munich's central Marienplatz to Starnberg and three other towns on the lake's west bank: Possenhofen, Feldafing, and Tutzing. The journey from Marienplatz to Starnberg takes 35 minutes. The east bank of the lake can be reached by bus from the town of Wolfratshausen, the end of the S-bahn 7 suburban line.

VISITOR INFORMATION

Fremdenverkehrsverband (⊠ Wittelsbacher Str. 9 [Am Kirchpl.], ☎ 08151/13008).

Wasserburg am Inn

Wasserburg floats like a faded ship of state in a benevolent, lazy loop of the Inn River, which comes within a few yards of cutting the ancient town off from the wooded slopes of the encroaching countryside. The river caresses the southern limits of the town center, embraces its eastern boundary with rocky banks 200 ft high, returns westward as if looking for a way out of this geographical puzzle, and then heads north in search of its final destination, the Danube. Wasserburg sleeps in its watery cradle, a perfectly preserved, beautifully set medieval town, once a vitally important trading post but later thankfully ignored by the industrialization that gripped Germany in the 19th century.

Exploring Wasserburg

You're never more than 100 yards or so from the river in Wasserburg's **Old Town** center, which huddles within the walls of the castle that originally gave Wasserburg (Water Castle) its name. The town has a southern, almost Italian look, typical of many Inn River towns. There are two large parking lots on the north and east banks, and you're advised to use one of them; the town council is expanding the traffic-free zone. It's only a few minutes' walk from the lots to central Marienplatz. There you'll find Wasserburg's late-Gothic brick **Town Hall.** ⊠ *Marienpl.* ☎ *DM 1.50.* ☉ *Guided tour Tues.–Fri. at 10, 11, 2, 3, and 4; weekends at 10 and 11.*

The 14th-century **Frauenkirche** on Marienplatz is the town's oldest church. It incorporates an ancient watchtower. The Baroque altar frames a beautiful Madonna by an unknown 14th-century artist.

Wasserburg's imposing 15th-century parish church, **St. Jakob,** has a finely crafted intricate Baroque pulpit, carved in 1640.

The **Erstes Imaginäres Museum,** at the town end of Wasserburg's only bridge, next to the 14th-century town gate, is one of Germany's most unusual museums. The museum has a collection of more than 400 world-famous paintings, without an original among them; every single one is a precise copy. ☎ *DM 3.* ☉ *May–Sept., Tues.–Sun. 11–5; Oct.–Apr., Tues.–Sun. 1–5.*

Wasserburg is a convenient base for enticing walks along the banks of the Inn River and into the surrounding countryside. A pretty path west leads to the village of **Attel.** Another half hour into the Attel River valley and one reaches the enchanting castle-restaurant of **Schloss Hart** (☎ 08039/1774).

Dining

The **Herrenhaus** (✉ Herrengasse 17, ☎ 08071/2800; $$) has the most compelling atmosphere for dining in Wasserburg—there's a centuries-old vaulted wine cellar. For simple and traditional Bavarian fare, try the **Gasthaus Zum Löwen** (✉ Marienpl. 10, ☎ 08071/7400; $$), a wood-paneled restaurant whose tables spill out onto the sidewalk in summer.

Lodging

Try the **Hotel Fletzinger** (✉ Fletzingergasse 1, D–83512, ☎ 08071/90890, FAX 08071/908–9177; $$) for solid comfort, along with antiques in some rooms, good, hearty food, and a beer garden. The old-fashioned **Hotel Paulaner-Stuben** (✉ Marienpl. 9, D–83512, ☎ 08071/3903, FAX 08071/50474; $) is housed behind the arcaded, rococo facade of one of Wasserburg's oldest and most historic buildings. Rooms, decorated in regal reds and blues, have every modern comfort.

Wasserburg A to Z

ARRIVING AND DEPARTING

By Car. Take the B–304 highway from Munich, which leads directly to Wasserburg. It's a 45-minute drive.

By Train. Take either the S-bahn 4 suburban line to Ebersberg and change to a local train to Wasserburg, or the Salzburg express, changing at Grafing Bahnhof to the local line. Both trips take 90 minutes.

VISITOR INFORMATION

Verkehrsamt (✉ Rathaus, Rathauspl. 1, ☎ 08071/1050).

GERMAN VOCABULARY

Basics

English	German	Pronunciation
Yes/no	Ja/nein	yah/nine
Please	Bitte	*bit*-uh
Thank you (very much)	Danke (vielen Dank)	*dahn*-kuh (*fee*-lun dahnk)
Excuse me	Entschuldigen Sie	ent-*shool*-de-gen zee
I'm sorry	Es tut mir leid.	es toot meer lite
Good day	Guten Tag	*goo*-ten tahk
Good bye	Auf Wiedersehen	auf *vee*-der-zane
Mr./Mrs.	Herr/Frau	hair/frau
Miss	Fräulein	*froy*-line
Pleased to meet	Sehr erfreut.	zair air-*froit*you.
How are you?	Wie geht es Ihnen?	vee *gate* es *ee*-nen?
Very well, thanks.	Sehr gut, danke.	zair goot *dahn*-kuh
And you?	Und Ihnen?	oont *ee*-nen

Numbers

1	ein(s)	eint(s)
2	zwei	tsvai
3	drei	dry
4	vier	fear
5	fünf	fumph
6	sechs	zex
7	sieben	*zee*-ben
8	acht	ahkt
9	neun	noyn
10	zehn	tsane

Days of the Week

Sunday	Sonntag	*zone*-tahk
Monday	Montag	*moan*-tahk
Tuesday	Dienstag	*deens*-tahk
Wednesday	Mittwoch	*mit*-voah
Thursday	Donnerstag	*doe*-ners-tahk
Friday	Freitag	*fry*-tahk
Saturday	Samstag/ Sonnabend	*zahm*-stakh/ *zonn*-a-bent

Useful Phrases

Do you speak English?	Sprechen Sie Englisch?	*shprek*-hun zee *eng*-glish?
I don't speak German.	Ich spreche kein Deutsch.	ich *shprek*-uh kine doych
Please speak slowly.	Bitte sprechen Sie langsam.	*bit*-uh *shprek*-en zee *lahng*-zahm
I am American/ British	Ich bin Amerikaner(in)/ Engländer(in)	ich bin a-mer-i-*kahn*-er(in)/ *eng*-glan-der(in)
My name is . . .	Ich heiße . . .	ich *hi*-suh
Yes please/No, thank you	Ja bitte/Nein danke	yah *bi*-tuh/*nine* dahng-kuh
Where are the restrooms?	Wo ist die Toilette?	vo ist dee twah-*let*-uh
Left/right	links/rechts	links/rechts
Open/closed	offen/geschlossen	O-fen/geh-*shloss*-en
Where is . . .	Wo ist . . .	*vo* ist
the train station?	der Bahnhof?	*dare bahn*-hof
the bus stop?	die Bushaltestelle?	dee *booss*-hahlt-uh-*shtel*-uh
the subway station?	die U-Bahn-Station?	dee oo-bahn-*staht*-sion
the airport?	der Flugplatz?	dare *floog*-plats
the post office?	die Post?	dee *post*
the bank?	die Bank?	dee *banhk*
the police station?	die Polizeistation?	dee po-lee-*tsai*-staht-sion
the American/ British consulate?	das amerikanische/ britische Konsulat?	dahs a-mare-i-*kahn*-ishuh/ *brit*-ish-uhcone-tso-*laht*
the Hospital?	das Krankenhaus?	dahs *krahnk*-en-house
the telephone	das Telefon	dahs te-le-*fone*
I'd like . . .	Ich hätte gairnhave . . .	ich *het*-uh gerne . . .
a room	ein Zimmer	I-nuh *tsim*-er
the key	den Schlüssel	den *shluh*-sul
a map	eine Stadtplan	I-nuh *staht*-plahn
a ticket	eine Karte	I-nuh *cart*-uh
How much is it?	Wieviel kostet das?	*vee*-feel *cost*-et dahs?
I am ill/sick	Ich bin krank	ich bin *krahnk*
I need . . .	Ich brauche . . .	ich *brow*-khuh
a doctor	einen Arzt	I-nen artst
the police	die Polizei	dee po-li-*tsai*
help	Hilfe	*hilf*-uh
Stop!	Halt!	hahlt
Fire!	Feuer!	*foy*-er
Look out/Caution!	Achtung!/Vorsicht!	*ahk*-tung/*for*-zicht

Dining Out

A bottle of . . .	eine Flasche . . .	I-nuh *flash*-uh
A cup of . . .	eine Tasse . . .	I-nuh *tahs*-uh
A glass of . . .	ein Glas . . .	ein glahss
Ashtray	der Aschenbecher	dare Ahsh-en-bekh-er
Bill/check	die Rechnung	dee *rekh*-nung
Do you have . . .?	Haben Sie . . .?	*hah*-ben zee
Food	Essen	*es*-en
I am a diabetic.	Ich bin Diabetiker(in)	ich bin dee-ah-*bet*-ik-er
I am on a diet.	Ich halte Diät.	ich *hahl*-tuh dee-*et*
I am a vegetarian.	Ich bin Vegetarier(in)	ich bin ve-guh-*tah*-re-er
I cannot eat . . .	Ich kann . . . nicht essen	ich kan . . . nicht *es*-en
I'd like to order . . .	Ich möchte . . .	ich *mohr*-shtuh bestellen buh-shtel-en . . .
Menu	die Speisekarte	dee *shpie*-zeh-car-tuh
Napkin	die Serviette	dee zair-vee-*eh*-tuh
Separate/all	Getrennt/alles	ge-*trent*/*ah*-les
together	zusammen	tsu-*zah*-men

MENU GUIDE

English	German
Made to order	Auf Bestellung
Side dishes	Beilagen
Extra charge	Extraaufschlag
When available	Falls verfügbar
Entrées	Hauptspeisen
Home made	Hausgemacht
(Not) included	. . .(nicht) inbegriffen
Depending on the season	je nach Saison
Local specialties	Lokalspezialitäten
Set menu	Menü
Lunch menu	Mittagskarte
Desserts	Nachspeisen
Style	. . . nach . . . Art
At your choice	. . . nach Wahl
At your request	. . . nach Wunsch
Prices are . . .	Preise sind . . .
Service included	*inklusive Bedienung*
Value added tax included	*inklusive Mehrwertsteuer (Mwst.)*
Specialty of the house	Spezialität des Hauses
Soup of the day	Tagessuppe
Appetizers	Vorspeisen
Is served from . . . to . . .	Wird von . . . bis . . . serviert

Breakfast

Bread	Brot
Roll(s)	Brötchen
Butter	Butter
Eggs	Eier
Hot	heiß
Cold	kalt
Decaffeinated	koffeinfrei
Jam	Konfitüre
Milk	Milch
Orange juice	Orangensaft
Scrambled eggs	Rühreier
Bacon	Speck
Fried eggs	Spiegeleier
White bread	Weißbrot
Lemon	Zitrone
Sugar	Zucker

Appetizers

Oysters	Austern
Frog legs	Froschschenkel
Goose liver paté	Gänseleberpastete
Lobster	Hummer
Shrimp	Garnelen
Crayfish	Krebs
Salmon	Lachs
Mussels	Muscheln
Prosciutto with melon	Parmaschinken mit Melone
Mushrooms	Pilze
Smoked . . .	Räucher . . .
Ham	Schinken
Snails	Schnecken
Asparagus	Spargel

Soups

Stew	Eintopf
Semolina dumpling soup	Grießnockerlsuppe
Goulash soup	Gulaschsuppe
Chicken soup	Hühnersuppe
Potato soup	Kartoffelsuppe
Liver dumpling soup	Leberknödelsuppe
Oxtail soup	Ochsenschwanzsuppe
Tomato soup	Tomatensuppe
Onion soup	Zwiebelsuppe

Methods of Preparation

Blue (boiled in salt and vinegar)	Blau
Baked	Gebacken
Fried	Gebraten
Steamed	Gedämpft
Grilled (broiled)	Gegrillt
Boiled	Gekocht
Sauteed	In Butter geschwenkt
Breaded	Paniert
Raw	Roh

When ordering steak, the English words "rare, medium, (well) done" are used and understood in German.

Fish and Seafood

Eel	Aal
Oysters	Austern
Trout	Forelle
Flounder	Flunder

Prawns	Garnelen
Halibut	Heilbutt
Herring	Hering
Lobster	Hummer
Scallops	Jakobsmuscheln
Cod	Kabeljau
Crab	Krabbe
Crayfish	Krebs
Salmon	Lachs
Spiny lobster	Languste
Mackerel	Makrele
Mussels	Muscheln
Red sea bass	Rotbarsch
Sole	Seezunge
Squid	Tintenfisch
Tuna	Thunfisch

Meats

Mutton	Hammel
Veal	Kalb(s)
Lamb	Lamm
Beef	Rind(er)
Pork	Schwein(e)

Cuts of Meat

Example: For "Lammkeule" see "Lamm" (above) + ". . . keule" (below)

Breast	. . . brust
Scallopini	. . . geschnetzeltes
Knuckle	. . . haxe
Leg	. . . keule
Liver	. . . leber
Tenderloin	. . . lende
Kidney	. . . niere
Rib	. . . rippe
Meat patty	Frikadelle
Meat loaf	Hackbraten
Cured pork ribs	Kasseler Rippchen
Liver meatloaf	Leberkäse
Ham	Schinken
Bacon and sausage with	Schlachtplattesauerkraut
Brawn	Sülze
Cooked beef with horseradish	and cream sauce

Game and Poultry

Duck	Ente
Pheasant	Fasan
Goose	Gans
Chicken	Hähnchen (Huhn)
Hare	Hase
Deer	Hirsch
Rabbit	Kaninchen
Capon	Kapaun
Venison	Reh
Pigeon	Taube
Turkey	Truthahn
Quail	Wachtel

Vegetables

Eggplant	Aubergine
Red cabbage	Blaukraut
Cauliflower	Blumenkohl
Beans	Bohnen
green	*grüne*
white	*weiße*
Button mushrooms	Champignons
Peas	Erbsen
Cucumber	Gurke
Cabbage	Kohl
Lettuce	Kopfsalat
Leek	Lauch
Asparagus, peas and carrots	Leipziger Allerlei
Corn	Mais
Carrots	Mohrrüben
Peppers	Paprika
Chanterelle mushrooms	Pfifferlinge
Mushrooms	Pilze
Brussels sprouts	Rosenkohl
Red beets	Rote Beete
Celery	Sellerie
Asparagus (tips)	Spargel(spitzen)
Tomatoes	Tomaten
Cabbage	Weißkohl
Onions	Zwiebeln
Spring Onions	Frühlingszwiebeln

Side dishes

Potato(s)	Kartoffel(n)
fried	*Brat . . .*
boiled in their jackets	*Pell . . .*
with parsley	*Petersilien . . .*
fried	*Röst . . .*
boiled in saltwater	*Salz . . .*
mashed	*. . . brei*
dumplings	*. . . klöße (knödel)*
pancakes	*. . . puffer*
salad	*. . . salat*
Pasta	Nudeln
French fries	Pommes frites
Rice	Reis
buttered	*Butter . . .*
steamed	*gedämpfter . . .*

Condiments

Basil	Basilikum
Vinegar	Essig
Spice	Gewürz
Garlic	Knoblauch
Herbs	Kräuter
Caraway	Kümmel
Bay leaf	Lorbeer
Horseradish	Meerettich
Nutmeg	Muskatnuß
Oil	Öl
Parsley	Petersilie
Saffron	Safran
Sage	Salbei
Chives	Schnittlauch
Mustard	Senf
Artificial sweetener	Süßstoff
Cinnamon	Zimt
Sugar	Zucker
Salt	Salz

Cheese

Mild	Allgäuer Käse, Altenburger (goat cheese), Appenzeller, Greyerzer, Hüttenkäse (cottage cheese), Kümmelkäse (with caraway seeds), Quark, Räucherkäse (smoked cheese), Sahnekäse (creamy), Tilsiter, Ziegekäse (goat cheese).
Sharp	Handkäse, Harzer Käse, Limburger.
Curd	frisch
Hard	hart
Mild	mild

Fruits

Apple	Apfel
Orange	Apfelsine
Apricot	Aprikose
Blueberry	Blaubeere
Blackberry	Brombeere
Strawberry	Erdbeere
Raspberry	Himbeere
Cherry	Kirsche
Grapefruit	Pampelmuse
Cranberry	Preiselbeere
Raisin	Rosine
Grape	Weintraube
Banana	Banane
Pear	Birne
Kiwi	Kiwi

Nuts

Peanuts	Erdnüsse
Hazelnuts	Haselnüsse
Coconut	Kokosnuß
Almonds	Mandeln
Chestnuts	Maronen

Desserts

Soufflé	. . . auflauf
Ice cream	. . . eis
Cake	. . . kuchen
Honey-almond cake	Bienenstich
Fruit cocktail	Obstsalat
Whipped cream	(Schlag)sahne
Black Forest cake	Schwarzwälder Kirschtorte

Drinks

Chilled	eiskalt
With/without ice	mit/ohne Eis
With/without water	mit/ohne Wasser
Straight	pur
Room temperature	Zimmertemperatur
Brandy	. . . geist
Distilled liquor	. . . korn
Liqueur	. . . likör
Schnapps	. . . schnaps
Egg liquor	Eierlikör
Mulled claret	Glühwein
Caraway-flavored liquor	Kümmel
Fruit brandy	Obstler
Vermouth	Wermut

When ordering a Martini, you have to specify "gin (vodka) and vermouth," otherwise you will be given a vermouth (Martini & Rossi).

Beer and Wine

Non-alcoholic	Alkoholfrei
A dark beer	Ein Dunkles
A light beer	Ein Helles
A mug (one quart)	Eine Maß
Draught	Vom Faß
Dark, bitter, high hops content	Altbier
Strong, high alcohol content	Bockbier (Doppelbock, Märzen)
Wheat beer with yeast	Hefeweizen
Light beer, strong hops aroma	Pils(ener)
Wheat beer	Weizen(bier)
Light beer and lemonade	Radlermaß
Wines	Wein
Rosé wine	Rosëwein
Red wine	Rotwein
White wine and mineral water	Schorle
Sparkling wine	Sekt

White wine	Weißwein
Dry	herb
Light	leicht
Sweet	süß
Dry	trocken
Full-bodied	vollmundig

Non-alcoholic Drinks

Coffee	Kaffee
decaffeinated	*koffeinfrei*
with cream/sugar	*mit Milch/Zucker*
with artificial sweetener	*mit Süßstoff*
black	*schwarz*
Lemonade	Limonade
orange	*Orangen . . .*
lemon	*Zitronen . . .*
Milk	Milch
Mineral water	Mineralwasser
carbonated/non-carbonated	*mit/ohne Kohlensäure*
Juice	*. . . saft*
(Hot) Chocolate	(heiße) Schokolade
Tea	Tee
iced tea	*Eistee*
herb tea	*Kräutertee*
with cream/lemon	*mit Milch/Zitrone*

INDEX

X = *restaurant*, 🏨 = *hotel*

NOTES

....
....
....
....
....
....
....
....
....
....
....
....
....
....
....
....
....
....
....
....
....
....
....
....
....
....
....
....
....
....

NOTES

NOTES

NOTES

With guidebooks for every kind of travel—from weekend
getaways to island hopping to adventures abroad—it's
easy to understand why smart travelers go with **Fodor's**.

Fodor's Travel Publications

Available at bookstores everywhere. For descriptions of all our titles, a key to Fodor's guidebook series, and on-line ordering, visit www.fodors.com/books

Gold Guides

U.S.

Alaska
Arizona
Boston
California
Cape Cod,
Martha's Vineyard,
Nantucket
The Carolinas &
Georgia
Chicago
Colorado

Florida
Hawai'i
Las Vegas, Reno,
Tahoe
Los Angeles
Maine, Vermont,
New Hampshire
Maui & Lāna'i
Miami & the Keys
New England
New Orleans

New York City
Oregon
Pacific North
Coast
Philadelphia & the
Pennsylvania
Dutch Country
The Rockies
San Diego
San Francisco

Santa Fe, Taos,
Albuquerque
Seattle &
Vancouver
The South
U.S. & British
Virgin Islands
USA
Virginia &
Maryland
Washington, D.C.

Foreign

Australia
Austria
The Bahamas
Belize &
Guatemala
Bermuda
Canada
Cancún, Cozumel,
Yucatán Peninsula
Caribbean
China
Costa Rica
Cuba
The Czech
Republic &
Slovakia
Denmark

Eastern &
Central Europe
Europe
Florence, Tuscany
& Umbria
France
Germany
Great Britain
Greece
Hong Kong
India
Ireland
Israel
Italy
Japan
London

Madrid &
Barcelona
Mexico
Montréal &
Québec City
Moscow,
St. Petersburg,
Kiev
The Netherlands,
Belgium &
Luxembourg
New Zealand
Norway
Nova Scotia, New
Brunswick, Prince
Edward Island
Paris
Portugal

Provence &
the Riviera
Scandinavia
Scotland
Singapore
South Africa
South America
Southeast Asia
Spain
Sweden
Switzerland
Thailand
Toronto
Turkey
Vienna & the
Danube Valley
Vietnam

Special-Interest Guides

Adventures to
Imagine
Alaska Ports of Call
Ballpark Vacations
The Best Cruises
Caribbean Ports
of Call
The Complete
Guide to America's
National Parks
Europe Ports of Call
Family Adventures
Fodor's Gay Guide
to the USA

Fodor's How to Pack
Great American
Learning Vacations
Great American
Sports & Adventure
Vacations
Great American
Vacations
Great American
Vacations
for Travelers
with Disabilities
Halliday's
New Orleans
Food Explorer

Healthy Escapes
Kodak Guide to
Shooting Great
Travel Pictures
National Parks
and Seashores
of the East
National Parks of
the West
Nights to Imagine
Orlando Like a Pro
Rock & Roll
Traveler Great
Britain and Ireland

Rock & Roll
Traveler USA
Sunday in San
Francisco
Walt Disney
World for Adults
Weekends in
New York
Wendy Perrin's
Secrets Every
Smart Traveler
Should Know
Worlds to Imagine

Fodor's Special Series

WHEREVER YOU TRAVEL, *H*ELP IS NEVER FAR AWAY.

From planning your trip to providing travel assistance along the way, American Express® Travel Service Offices are always there to help you do more.

Munich

Reiseland American Express (R)
Promenadenplatz 6
At Hotel Bayerischerhof
(48) (89) 290900

Travel
www.americanexpress.com/travel

American Express Travel Service Offices are located throughout Germany.